Y0-BUB-465

# RELIGION IN SOVIET RUSSIA

# RELIGION
## IN
# SOVIET RUSSIA
### *1917-1942*

### *by* N. S. TIMASHEFF

*Assistant Professor of Sociology,
Fordham University*

**GREENWOOD PRESS, PUBLISHERS**
WESTPORT, CONNECTICUT

Library of Congress Cataloging in Publication Data

Timasheff, Nicholas Sergeyevitch, 1886-1970.
    Religion in Soviet Russia, 1917-1942.

    Reprint of the ed. published by Sheed and Ward,
New York.
        Bibliography: p.
        Includes index.
        1.  Christianity--Russia.  2.  Church and state in
Russia--1917-      I.  Title.
BR936.T5  1979      209'.47      78-23615
ISBN 0-313-21040-3

# LIBRARY
The University of Texas
At San Antonio

# Foreword

THE PURPOSE OF THIS WORK is to give some notion of the assault on religion which has taken place in Russia during the last twenty-five years, of the magnificent resistance of the believers, and of the situation brought about by repeated onslaughts and repulses. A history of the stubborn resistance of a nation to the spiritual oppression of its rulers may, in part, explain the resistance of the Russian people to foreign aggression.

The sources of this work are, first, data published in Soviet newspapers and journals; second, observations made by competent foreign visitors to Russia; and, in a few specified cases, my own personal observations during the years 1917–21 which I spent in Petrograd; finally, private communications which have reached me from reliable sources. The events of the earlier years have many times been described: here their history is only reproduced on broad lines, and to whatever extent was necessary for the reconstruction of main tendencies; references to sources have been made whenever controversial questions or little known details were involved. The last phase, which has not yet been systematically treated in any work, is described copiously, and source references are as complete as possible.

I have published, in several languages, papers on the religious situation in Russia and related subjects. These papers were written after a careful study of first-hand material, but, because of the conditions of publication, it was not always possible to refer to the individual sources. Today these sources (which I used in Prague and Paris) are not accessible. It is even probable that a number of papers which I consulted have not been preserved in any library outside Russia. In all such cases, reference is made to my previous papers.

This work could never have been written without the encouragement and help of my wife, Tatiana N. Timasheff. To her and to Rev. Moorhouse Millar, S. J., who greatly helped me in editing the manuscript, I am deeply indebted. Also I wish to express my thanks to the editors of *Thought* and of *The Russian Review* for their kind permission to reprint in this work parts of articles which appeared originally in their journals.

N. S. TIMASHEFF,
*Fordham University*

March 19, 1942

# Preface

THIS IS NOT just another book about Russia. Like many that have preceded it, it deals with existing conditions under the Communist regime. But the angle from which Dr. Timasheff has undertaken to make an estimate of those conditions differs sharply from the usual approach of those whose standard of measurement has been either the theoretic soundness of Communist assumptions, on the one hand, or the success or failure of the Communist experiment, considered merely in its social and economic aspect, on the other. As will be noticed, he has, throughout the following pages, sedulously avoided all direct criticism of Communism in Russia on either of these grounds, and this with a view to raising the much more important issue, so far as the Russian people themselves are concerned, namely the question as to how Christianity in Russia has actually fared during the last twenty-five years, at the hands of those who have manifestly attempted everything a perverted ingenuity could devise to obliterate it from the hearts and memory of one of the most religiously minded people in our present day world.

In order to make his point the more effectively Dr. Timasheff has confined himself to a simple, straightforward and authentic account of the religious situation in Russia based upon the most unimpeachable evidence possible, short of personal observation, that is to say, evidence grudgingly supplied by the religious persecutors themselves. As a result we are presented with a state of facts which is bound to be surprising to those who, through propaganda methods or otherwise, have been led to identify the existing Russian people, as a whole, with such abstract notions as "The Communists," "The Reds," or "The Soviets," which is about as accurate and sensible as it would be if we in the United States found ourselves constantly referred to as "The New Dealers" instead of Americans.

In other words, instead of the caricatures, favorable or unfavorable, that have been shaping public opinion with regard to conditions in Russia, we have here a firsthand portrayal of the Communist government and its agents, atheistic in principle and hyper-modernistic in their anti-traditional and exclusive emphasis upon economic expertizing and technology, confronted by two living and active factors that modernists generally, throughout the world, had come to believe might well be left out of all further reckoning. These two factors are fundamental human nature, which, in the long run, always tends to rise above the level of error and deceit, and the supernatural faith of a people sustained and strengthened, even to the point of heroism, by sacramental means administered by a hierarchy that derives its sacred orders from Christ and the Apostles.

Many a passage in which Dr. Timasheff has recorded how, without any trace of fanaticism but in the spirit of a genuine Christian humility and fortitude, the Russian faithful have confounded the persecutor, to the point of forcing him to admit the failure of his best efforts, reads like a page from the history of the early Christians in the days of the Roman Empire.

MOORHOUSE F. X. MILLAR, S. J.

# Selected Bibliography

The best works on the religious situation in Russia prior to the Revolution are: N. M. ZERNOFF, Moscow, *The Third Rome*, London, 1937; J. S. CURTISS, *State and Church in Russia, 1900–17*, New York, 1939; and P. N. MILIUKOFF, *Outlines of Russian Culture*, part I, Philadelphia, 1942.

The best work on the philosophy of Communism is C. MAC-FADDEN, *The Philosophy of Communism*, New York, 1939. Lenin's papers on religion have been collected in a pamphlet translated into English under the title *Lenin on Religion*, New York, 1935. An interpretation of the Russian revolution as a metamorphosis of the Russian religious spirit is given by N. BERDYAEV, *The Origin of Russian Communism*, London, 1936, and F. STEPUN, *Das Antlitz Russlands and das Gesicht der Revolution*, Bern, 1934.

The earlier period (up to 1928) has been described by F. MacCULLAGH, *The Bolshevik Persecution of Christianity*, New York, 1924; A. A. VALENTINOFF, *The Assault of Heaven*, London, 1925; M. SPINKA, *The Church and the Russian Revolution*, New York, 1927; J. F. HECKER, *Christianity and Communism*, New York, 1927; W. C. EMHARDT, *Religion in Soviet Russia*, London, 1928; and G. P. FEDOTOFF, *The Russian Church Since the Revolution*, London, 1928.

The later period (up to 1936) has been described by G. MECKLENBURG, *Russia Challenges Religion*, New York, 1934; A. KELLER, *Church and State on the European Continent*, London, 1936; and M. SPINKA, *Christianity Confronts Communism*, New York, 1939.

The best works on anti-religious propaganda are: M. D'HERBIGNY, *Militant Atheism*, London, 1933; and L. CAPUCCIO, *Russia regno del'anticristo*, Milano, 1933. The official standpoint has been expressed by Y. YAROSLAVSKY, *Religion in the USSR*, London, 1932.

ix

# Abbreviations

To avoid a tedious repetition of transliterated Russian words, the titles of Russian newspapers and journals (to which more than incidental references have been made) have been replaced by the following symbols:

A.  *Antireligioznik* (the Antireligious, monthly organ of the Militant Atheists League).

B.  *Bezbozhnik* (The Godless, a popular publication of the same League, appearing every ten days).

B.(m)  *Bezbozhnik* (monthly edition of the preceding).

I.  *Izvestia* (News, official paper of the Soviet government).

K.G.  *Krasnaya Gazeta* (The Red Paper, evening paper appearing in Leningrad).

K.P.  *Komsomolskaya Pravda* (The Truth of the Comsomol, official paper of the Young Communist League).

L.P.  *Leningradskaya Pravda* (The Truth of Leningrad, official paper of the Leningrad Committee of the Communist Party).

P.  *Pravda* (The Truth, official paper of the Central Committee of the Communist Party).

P.S.  *Partiinoye Stroitelstvo* (The Construction of the Party; a monthly publication of the same Committee).

S.Z.  *Sotsialisticheskoye Zemledelye* (Socialist Agriculture, daily paper of the Commissariat of Agriculture).

T.  *Trud* (Labor, daily paper of the Central Committee of the Trade Unions).

U.G.  *Uchitelskaya Gazeta* (The Teacher's Paper, daily paper of the Commissariat for Education).

xi

V.C.  *Volzhskaya Kommuna* (The Volga Commune, official paper of the Samara, now Kuibysheff, Committee of the Communist Party).

V.M.  *Vechernyaya Moskva* (Evening Moscow, an evening paper appearing in Moscow).

V.P.  *Voprossy Profdvizeniya* (Problems of the Labor Movement, monthly organ of the Central Committee of the Trade Unions).

Z.K.P.  *Za Kommunisticheskoye Prosvescheniye* (For Communist Education, official paper of the Commissariat for Education).

# Contents

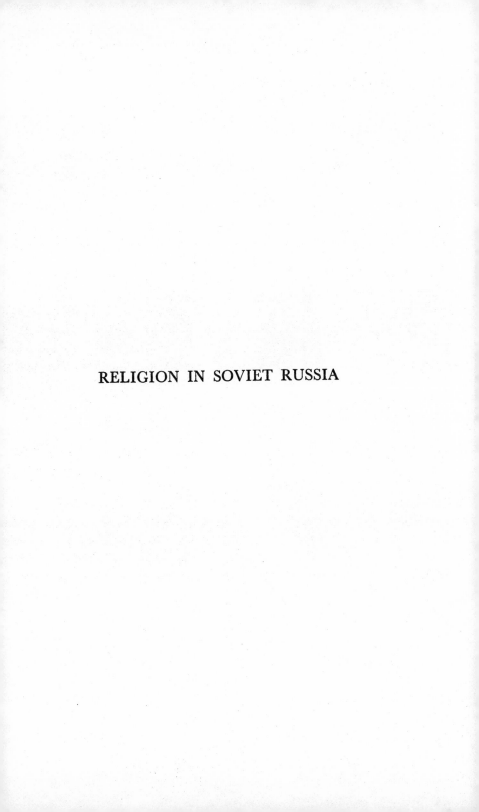

RELIGION IN SOVIET RUSSIA

# CHAPTER ONE

# The Inevitable Conflict

I

In the Fall of 1917, the Communists were in possession of Russia. To the Russian people this meant much more than a change in rulers: it was an historical catastrophe of unprecedented magnitude. For the Communists were militant atheists who not only rejected God but considered every religion an enemy to be exterminated as quickly as possible.

On the other hand, the country which they controlled was a nation where, for centuries, Christianity in its Greek Orthodox form had been one of the fundamental principles of life. The identification of "Russian" and "Greek Orthodox" was common. From time immemorial, the Russian peasant had called himself "krestianin," i.e., Christian.[1]

Thus the Communists' rise to power created a tragic conflict which affected not only religion, but life in all its aspects. It was a war between national tradition and international Utopia, and, in regard to religion, the clash of two faiths. The twenty-four years which have elapsed since the cataclysm of 1917 have been years of ceaseless struggle and difficult adjustment. In this work, the religious aspect of the struggle and the adjustment will be examined. It must be introduced by a summary description of the two camps, Orthodoxy and Communism, as they were at the

1

beginning of their conflict, and by a short discussion of the problem of how militant atheists could master a Christian nation.

2

Russia was Christianized in 988, and so became a member of the then undivided Church. Since she had received Christianity from Byzantium, and for many years was ruled by "Greek" bishops, she quite naturally followed Byzantium when, 66 years later, the great schism divided Christendom into two parts. From Byzantium the young Russian Church borrowed her leaning towards caesaropapism, a form of State-Church relationship which all but unites the two powers under the actual supremacy of the secular.[2] In Byzantium and later in Russia, the monarch at his coronation was held to receive a share in the spiritual power, an honor which was indicated by privileges he was granted at Divine Service.

The growth of Russia and its Church, and the parallel decline of Byzantium, resulted in the Church's emancipation: in the fifteenth century it was recognized as "autocephalous" and joined, as a new member, the federation of National Churches which compose Eastern or Greek Orthodoxy. In 1589, about a century and a half after the fall of Byzantium, the Russian primate assumed the title of Patriarch.

Emancipation did not involve any change in the structure of the State-Church dichotomy: the Church remained closely allied with the Grand Duchy, later with the Czardom of Moscow to whose victory and final elevation to uncontested supremacy it had greatly contributed. In the course of centuries, some fluctuations naturally took place. In the seventeenth century, for about fifty years, the principle of dualism prevailed, making the State and Church equal partners; this was manifested in the practice of enacting laws under the joint signatures of the Czar and the Patriarch. However, this structure was the result of certain accidental circumstances, especially the simultaneous rule of able Patriarchs and of relatively mild and weak Czars. A short conflict between the Czar and the Patriarch resulted in a restoration of the traditional order, i.e., the supremacy of the Czar.

Until the sixteenth century, the Russian State had almost no trouble with non-conformists or non-Christians. After the conquest of the realms of Kazan and Astrakhan (1552 and 1557), a number of Mahomedans became subjects of the Orthodox Czar. The State assumed an attitude at once tolerant and discriminating: no one was persecuted for worshipping Allah and Mahomet, but it was understood that non-conformists could not hope for any political office in the Orthodox State. When, in 1667, the schism of the Raskol took place,[3] another formula was easily found to deal with the situation: whoever was born in the Orthodox Church could not legally forsake it.

Although closely united to the State, the Church was still a semi-autonomous body of great strength, endowed with considerable material means and prestige. Then came the reforms of Peter the Great (1682–1725) which tended towards the Westernization of Russia, and which were opposed by the traditionalists, among them a great many high Church officials. Anxious to make his reforms final, Peter committed an error of incalculable consequences: he used his supremacy in the Church to abolish the Patriarchal See and created, in its place, a Synod patterned on the organization of the Lutheran Church of Prussia and Sweden. The Synod was a college of bishops, convoked by the Procurator General, a government official of ministerial rank, and was consequently dependent upon him. No change in dogma or rites was made, but the Church lost every vestige of independence and became subservient to the State. Half a century later, the Empress Catherine II, a German, secularized almost all of the Church estates and for compensation granted a State allowance. The subordination of the Church was almost complete.

The territorial acquisitions of Peter the Great and of his successors, particularly of Catherine II, added to the subjects of the Czars (now called Emperors) millions of Roman Catholics, in Lithuania and the Polish provinces, and of Protestants in the Baltic provinces; at the same time about half of the Jews in the world became subjects of a State which, up to the middle of the eighteenth century, had not permitted them to enter its territory!

Very complicated legislation was gradually evolved to regulate these conditions. According to this, the Greek Orthodox was the Established Church, morally and materially supported by the State, but also completely dependent upon it. Religious propaganda was permitted only to its members, and no person born of Greek Orthodox parents could ever change his religion. Other recognized religions formed a hierarchy, with the Roman Catholic, the Lutheran, the Reformed and the Armenian Churches at the top, Islam in the middle, and the Hebrew at the bottom. Tolerance was the official attitude of the State toward these religions: no one was reproved for belonging to them if his parents had belonged; but religious propaganda was forbidden and discrimination was shown toward their members. In practice, Lutherans were on an equal footing with Orthodox, whereas the Catholics, especially in the Western, formerly Polish provinces, were handicapped and the Hebrews were almost completely debarred from administrative positions, greatly restricted in professional careers, and forbidden to live outside the "Pale of Settlement." [4] After these came dissenters, i.e., the "old ritualists," and the non-recognized Protestant sects who were sometimes treated with an arbitrary brutality.[5]

Thus, a sort of official hierarchy of religions was created. But, in addition to the hierarchy, there was a protective attitude towards religion in general. Religious education was obligatory in all schools, both public and private, and was given by clergymen of the denomination of their pupils. The State recognized only religious marriage and divorce, so that, according to their Church's rules, no divorce could be granted in Russia to Roman Catholics; and Greek Orthodox divorces were extremely rare. Open anti-religious propaganda was not tolerated.

This order appeared to be extremely favorable to the Greek Orthodox Church and partly it was so. But protection against external competition resulted quite naturally in internal weakness. The Church never participated in any kind of social activity. The training given in seminaries was second-rate; it is true that many graduates received advanced courses at the theological academies whose standards were high; but graduates from the academies were usually appointed to city parishes, and the priests assigned to the countryside were often men of inferior moral and intellectual fiber. Furthermore, lack of competition stimulated the development of a tendency inherited by the Russian Church from Byzantium: this was an emphasis on ritualism, on words and gestures often insufficiently understood. This was the feature which most often struck foreign observers who were unable to detect the simple but vivid religious sentiments of the people performing these rites or the significance of the "Orthodox way of life," i.e., a set of customs closely bound up with Church holidays, Lenten fasts, etc. Never were these ways of life considered restricting or limiting; on the contrary, they were felt to be as natural and unbreakable as folkways. Pilgrimages to monasteries or even to the Holy Land were common, and a bequest of money to the Church or to some specified pious memorials was a customary item in the wills of the well-to-do, especially merchants.

After granting the Orthodox Church full protection, the State did not feel obliged to allow it very ample means. The Church in Russia was never so rich as was frequently assumed by its antagonists, both Russian and foreign; cash was gathered for the most part from the voluntary contributions of members. A careful analysis of the Church income for 1900 has shown that, from a total of 122 million rubles, only twenty-three million came from the State, the rest was made up from other sources.[6] In the countryside, the priests as a rule did not receive salaries; they were given plots of land which they tilled as their parishioners did; for the rest, they depended on the fees for baptisms, weddings, burials, and special prayers, an irritating levy which tended to set the people against their priests. In addition, the State provided the sons of priests with a free education in theological seminaries. This ended in making the clergy a kind of hereditary caste which included many priests who chose ecclesiastical careers not because of vocation but because of their specialized training.

For protection the Greek Orthodox Church paid the heavy price of subordination and this subordination increasingly weakened her position when, for reasons which cannot be discussed here, a persistent antagonism developed between the State and the "intelligentsia." The opposition to the State was so complete and so bitter that all forces allied with the State or submissive to it became suspect and even hateful to the intelligentsia: in the Church these persons abhorred "the State administration of ecclesiastical affairs," an unhappy phrase sometimes used in official correspondence to designate the Synod and the diocesan consistories. A number of authors, artists, academic teachers, professional men, not to mention professional revolutionists, a group which appeared around 1870, became violent atheists: for religious indifference, so frequent among Western liberals, had been almost unknown in Russia. And as information about Russia came to foreigners through the intellectuals, a fiction of the complete decay of the Orthodox Church was everywhere accepted outside the country.

However, the extent of decline should not be exaggerated. The peasantry,[7] numerically the largest group of the Russian population, remained faithful to the Church and continued to perform its rites and to live in the "Orthodox way." Nor did the flight from the Church draw all the intellectuals of the country: the Slavophiles and their followers maintained their allegiance; the two greatest writers of the later nineteenth century, Dostoyevsky and Tolstoy, were highly religious men, the former, a faithful member of the Orthodox Church, the latter inclined toward Protestantism.

Early in the twentieth century the situation was much improved. Among the liberal decrees of the period of the abortive revolution of 1905–06, that of April 17, 1905 repealed the statutes which forbade members of the Orthodox Church to join other denominations, promoted a large number of the "old ritualists" to the rank of "protected denominations" and substantially curbed the persecution of the rest. Influential intellectuals were reconciled to the State after the Constitutional reform of 1905–06, and this signified also their reconciliation to the Church. In 1909, a symposium entitled "Vekhi" was published by a group of intellectual leaders who here recanted their materialistic and atheistic views and professed their belief in idealism. Clubs for the discussion of religious and philosophical problems were created in the main centers of the country, and attendance at their meetings was high. Certain historians and art critics became interested in the history of the icon and Church architecture and rediscovered ecclesiastical glory in the Russian past. A better understanding of the unhappy predicament of the Church arose among intellectuals and enlightened clergymen who realized the necessity of liberating the Church from State tutelage.

The revival did not come to full maturity because of the resistance of the last emperor. The overthrow of the Imperial government (March, 1917) and the liberal attitude of the Provisional government allowed Church reform to proceed. A national council called in Moscow restored the

Patriarchal See and provided for more vigorous parochial life. However, the reforms came too late: they could be put into practice only after the overthrow of the Provisional government by the Communists (November, 1917) and in an atmosphere of impending persecution.

Thus, for the most part, the Church had to meet persecution in a state of internal weakness. To many observers this Church appeared to be exactly as it was described by the Communists: "prostituted to the autocratic government," [8] a nuisance, an obstacle to progress, a corpse to be buried. Certainly, it was nothing of the sort. There was religious life behind the petrified external structure; there was faith in the flock; there was devotion and a readiness for sacrifice.

How can we know this? Faith certainly cannot be observed and measured by the yardstick of behaviorism; but three facts are explained if we assume that the Russian Church was alive and cannot be explained if we consider that it was dead.

First, as has already been shown, the Russian Orthodox Church was mainly supported by voluntary gifts from its members. Does this not prove that for them the Church was something more than the "administration of religious affairs"?

Second, when emigrating from Russia, before and after the revolution, Russian people did not forget the faith of their fathers and did their best to set up the Church in their new homes. Yet they were altogether free to abandon it along with political allegiance to the old country.[9]

Third, twenty-four years of persecution and the withdrawal of any external support did not destroy religion in Russia. There are even symptoms of religious revival, and as revival is impossible without survival, this means that, before war and revolution, there had been true religious life, and that the Church was something more than a conglomeration of Byzantine rites, sustained by the machinery of Czarist autocracy. The survival and revival will be discussed in one of the later chapters of this work (see Chapter III). It may be asserted now that in attacking religion the Communists attacked something that meant much to the millions of people subjected to their rule.

### 3

Communist doctrines were imported into Russia as part of the great process of Westernization. Isolated Marxian thinkers appeared in Russia in the 70's of the nineteenth century, but it was not until the 90's that a "Social Democratic Party of Russia" was created by a few resolute men who challenged the vigilance of the Imperial police. In 1903 the party, which then comprised a few thousand men, split into two wings: the Mensheviks (moderate) and the Bolsheviks (radical), the latter under Lenin's leadership. The name of Communist Party was only taken by the group after the decisive victory of 1917.

The doctrine of Communism is orthodox Marxism.[10] And Marxism is much more than a political theory or a social ideal: it is a comprehensive philosophy of life which includes an epistemology, a metaphysics, a philosophy of history (which today we would call sociology), an applied theory of revolution, and a social ideal. The metaphysical foundation of Marxism is materialism: matter and its motion is all that actually exists; consciousness is determined by material existence and is its product or modification. Marx and his disciples had evolved these propositions by intuition, mainly by a dialectic in the style of Hegel who was in vogue when they were young. Then masses of facts were accumulated and explained in the light of Marxist theory; whether *all* known social facts could be thus explained was not taken into consideration. Today attempts are made to give Marxism an idealistic interpretation,[11] for crude materialism is no longer fashionable. Such compromises are irrelevant to this study; the Russian Marxists accepted orthodox materialism, insisted on it and contributed to its refinement. In their philosophy of history the material character of all that exists is used as the basis for an economic interpretation of social processes. Economic conditions and relations are established and altered "independently of human will." They form the "substructure" of every society and are reflected in human brains by vague images: morals, religion, metaphysics and other forms of "ideology" which form the "superstructure" of society. Their independence is merely superficial; actually they have no history at all, they have no development: as economic conditions change, so change the products of thought, including religion (F. Engels, *Anti-Duehring*). Marxists try to prove this assertion by the method of concomitant changes; in their opinion great religious changes have reflected decisive economic changes: "When the ancient world was in its last throes, the ancient religions were overcome by Christianity. When Christian ideas succumbed in the 18th century to rationalist ideas, feudal society fought its death battle with the then revolutionary bourgeoisie. The ideas of religious liberty and freedom of conscience gave expression to the sway of free competition within the domain of knowledge" (*Communist Manifesto*).

In this way the subordinate role of religion in the social process is "proved." Then they proceed further and try to establish the nefarious role of religion in society. "All religion is nothing else than the fantastic reflection, in the minds of men, of those external forces which dominate their everyday existence, a reflection in which the earthly forces assume the form of supernatural forces" (Engels, *Anti-Duehring*). "The omnipotence of God is nothing but the fantastic reflection of the impotence of people before nature and the economic relations created by themselves" (Marx, *Capital*).

When applied to capitalist society in which the fathers of Marxism lived, this general theory pigeonholes religion as one of the instruments of oppression which make capitalism so hateful to socialists, especially to Marxists. "Fear created the Gods," said Lenin, "fear before the force of capitalism which is blind. On every step the life of the proletarian and that of the petty employer is threatened and leads to sudden, unexpected ruin, to calamities which turn them into beggars and prostitutes and end in death from starvation—these are the roots of contemporary religion." Expanding an idea which Marx had expressed in the famous slogan "religion is an opiate for the people," Lenin said: "Being born from dull suppression . . . religion teaches those who toil in poverty to be resigned and patient in this world, and consoles them with the hope of reward in heaven. As for those who live upon the labor of others, religion teaches them to be charitable, thus providing a justification for the exploiters to sympathize with religion." And furthermore: "The oppression of humanity by religion is but the product and reflex of economic oppression within society."

Thus it appears that, in Marxist theory, religion cannot be separated from the class structure of society. The "liberation of humanity" from this structure is the ultimate end of socialism; therefore, religion must be destroyed. In Lenin's words, "All contemporary religions and churches, all and every kind of religious organization, Marxism has always viewed as instruments of bourgeois reaction, serving as a defense of exploitation and the doping of the working class. . . . The struggle against religion cannot be limited to abstract ideological preachery . . . this struggle should be brought into connection with the concrete practice of the class movement directed towards the elimination of the social roots of religion. . . . The party of the proletariat must be the spiritual leader in the struggle against all kinds of medievalism, including the official religion."

Might not this struggle be lessened or even abandoned, if religion were transformed and adapted to "progress"? [12] "No," said Lenin, "there can be no good religion, or perhaps better religion is still more dangerous than poor religion." If man is to be made happy, religion must be destroyed. And this is not all. In a classless society religion can no longer exist. For religion is merely a reflection of external forces, and with capitalism, the last external force, it will disappear.

Before their rise to power, the Communists were well aware of the fact that they were a long way from the classless society of their dreams, and that during an intermediary period the problem of undermining religion had to be solved. So long as they were a small minority party within a semi-feudal State (this was the Marxist diagnosis of Imperial Russia), they had to introduce into their program the idea of the "separation of Church and State," and hope that the realization of this demand would better expose the Church to their attacks. This point seemed to be in conformity with the ideas of the moderate socialists, *e.g.*, of the German Social Democrats who included in their program the catch-phrase, religion is the private business of each individual. Lenin never interpreted things in that way. To him the demand that the State declare religion "a private affair" did not mean that, for the party, the problem of fighting the dope of the people, religious superstition, was a private affair.

Once in power, the relative moderation of the previous program was no longer necessary: the uncompromising antipathy of the Party to all religion was very soon exposed in words and deeds. But obviously, this is a subject to be treated in the next chapter.

### 4

A wide gulf separated Communism and Holy Russia in the countryside. Nevertheless, the masses gave power to the Communists. That this was so should not be denied: whereas power in the capital was acquired by a *coup d'état* against a government (the Provisional government) which believed in the magic of words and had no understanding of reality, the quick expansion of the authority of the new government throughout the country and its ability to defeat all antagonists cannot be explained unless popular support is allowed, at least in the first few months.

This popular support seems to be a puzzle. The puzzle cannot be solved if the particular situation in Russia, A.D. 1917, is considered in isolation. Perhaps it can be if the following more general ideas, which have been drawn from a study of other revolutionary movements, are applied.

When a country reaches a "pre-revolutionary situation" —and such a situation was created in Russia by the inability of the Imperial government to adjust the country to the conditions of a modern war—society becomes plastic. Whereas in "organic" or static periods, what will be to-morrow can be predicted from what was yesterday; in revolutionary periods this cannot be done: men seem to stand at a crossroad and to have to choose between two or more directions of advance. These directions usually are personified by groups, or parties, and their leaders, and the decision depends on the outcome of competition between these groups.

In such competition two factors give victory. The first is the adequacy of the promises made by the party to the momentary desires of the groups whose support is decisive; the second factor is the relative ability for leadership.

If, in a concrete case, these two conflict, a long and complicated struggle ensues. If they coincide (and for reasons not to be discussed here, they usually do), their lucky possessors are victorious.

This is almost obvious and would not be contested. But a further statement must be made about a little known factor in revolutions: if, for reasons just discussed, a group or leader acquires power, then this group or leader is able to realize not only those elements of the program which gave them power, but also a part, at least, of the residue, i.e., those points which were not at issue during the period of competition.

This is possible in the beginning only in regard to those points on the program which are not directly contradictory to both the immediate and the permanent desires of the masses. Gradually, with the consolidation of the new order created by the revolution, this limitation disappears. As society is no longer plastic, the rules concerning revolutionary periods no longer obtain. This analysis shows, incidentally, the fallacy in the commonly accepted notion that every nation has the government it likes (this is the basis of the principle of non-interference): if the government is dictatorial (and revolutionary governments usually are), the nation has the government which it liked during the revolutionary crisis; whether it continues to like it will be decided during the next revolutionary crisis when once more society has become plastic.

Let us now apply this theory to the victory of the Communists in Russia. In 1917 Russian society was highly plastic. In the competition for power, the Communists offered the most appealing slogans; while the liberal and moderate socialist parties spoke of such abstract things as democracy and international pacification, the Communists concentrated their propaganda on four points:

(1) peace, i.e., the immediate cessation of a war whose ends were never sufficiently understood by the masses;

(2) land, i.e., the immediate gratification of the peasants' longing to have the landlords' estates divided among them;

(3) bread, i.e., the immediate alleviation of the food crisis in the major cities, and

(4) "all power to the Soviets," which was interpreted as the abolition of bureaucracy, direct rule by the masses, and

the likelihood of the cessation of taxation and compulsory military service.

Neither the dictatorial structure of the future State (in accordance with Lenin's idea of leadership), nor the organized attack on religion was ever mentioned in the propaganda. The prevalence of atheist or at least agnostic sentiments in the majority of the other parties which were struggling for power explains the fact that the anti-religious attitude of the Communists was not used by their opponents to defeat them.

Moreover, one cannot deny that efficient leadership was the keynote of the Communist Party. This party had evolved according to a pattern of semi-military subordination to the leader and of blind acceptance of the Party doctrine; the leader himself possessed a genius for correctly diagnosing concrete situations and for drawing realistic conclusions from his premises; many excellent organizers and able propagandists (among them Trotsky) assisted him. The structure of the other parties was democratic; none was headed by a person whose ascendancy was beyond question; and none of them had that intuitive understanding of reality which was so eminent in Lenin. They concentrated all attention upon squabbling among themselves and fighting off the imaginary bugbear of monarchical restoration; they completely overlooked the possibility of a Communist *coup d'état*. They possessed brilliant speakers, but their propaganda was addressed to fictitious "revolutionary masses" which, according to their books, ought to have existed. They had no eyes for the living men and women who, if they had been sensibly approached, might have become their supporters.

The combination of these factors explains the victory of the Communists. Once in power, they began to put into effect parts of their program that had not been advertised in the course of the struggle and for which there was consequently no popular ratification. So long as their measures were limited to the expropriation of riches accumulated by the upper classes of the defunct Imperial society, there was no direct opposition to popular wishes. Meanwhile, the new order was consolidated; the period of plasticity was over and Russia could be remoulded on the lines of Marxism. This no longer coincided with the wishes of large sections of the population, but for the rulers this was no longer important; for a *non-plastic society must endure the government which it chose during the preceding crisis!*

Similar explanations might be given to a number of events which took place in the course of the Fascist revolutions in Italy and Germany, but this would be a long digression. On the other hand, this explanation of the Russian puzzle is preferable to more sophisticated explanations which see in the anti-religious fanaticism of Communism a kind of metamorphosis of the rooted piety of the Russian national spirit; [13] this point of view would compel us to think of the victory of Communism as a straight continuation of Russian history, which it certainly was not. That it never was is today conclusively proved by the development of Communist society in the last few years, a development which tends toward a compromise between National Tradition and the Communist Utopia and even a partial reconciliation of the atheist government to religion. But this is the end of our story. It begins with religion's reckless persecution.

## FOOTNOTES TO CHAPTER ONE

(1) In contrast to the Western identification of rural people and heathens, shown in the term "pagans". Because of phonetic coincidence, the term *krestiane* may also be derived from the Russian word for cross, which is *krest*.

(2) The Greek Orthodox Church does not ascribe any dogmatic value to caesaropapism; for centuries, Greek Orthodox Churches have existed under Moslem rule, and during the last few centuries also within Roman Catholic States (Poland, Austria, Hungary).

(3) The schism took place in 1667 after Patriarch Nikon had ordered the correction of liturgical books and some rites, in which the Russian Church had mistakenly departed from the standards of Greek Orthodoxy. A number of believers refused to follow the Patriarch and maintained their "old" books, rites and icons; later on they were called "old-ritualists" (the usual translation "old believers" is misleading).

(4) It is noteworthy that discrimination against Jews was purely religious and not racial.

(5) Some extreme groups evolved beliefs and rites which would have been suppressed in any country. It is noteworthy that the *Dukhobory,* after their emigration to the New World, caused much trouble.

(6) J. S. Curtiss, *Church and State in Russia,* 1900–1917, (New York, 1940), pp. 128 ff.

(7) In 1914, the rural population formed 81.6% of the total population of Russia. *Cf.* N. S. Timasheff, "The Population of Soviet Russia," *Rural Sociology,* Vol. 5, 1940, p. 305.

(8) J. F. Hecker, *Religion Under the Soviets* (New York, 1927), p. 29.

(9) In the United States, Russians from Russia proper and parts of the former Austro-Hungarian monarchy, have built up a Church comprising 350 parishes, 11 bishops and a Metropolitan.

(10) The cursory review of Marxist philosophy which follows in the text consists of direct quotations and adaptations from the fundamental works of Marx and Engels, as well as from Lenin's papers collected in a special pamphlet (see Selected Bibliography). The best presentation of Marxist philosophy is by MacFadden, *The Philosophy of Communism* (New York, 1939).

(11) See, for instance, S. Hook, *Towards the Understanding of Karl Marx* (New York, 1933). After 1925, the official doctrine of the Communist Party in Russia shifted from old fashioned "mechanical materialism" to a more sophisticated "dialectical materialism" which

considers that the term "matter" simply designates all that is submitted to change.

(12) Such ideas were expressed by several Russian Communists, shortly before the outbreak of the war of 1914; prominent among them was Lunacharsky, later Commissar for Education.

(13) Such explanations are given by some Russian philosophers, among them Berdyaeff and Stepun (see Selected Bibliography).

# CHAPTER TWO

# The Attack On Religion

## I

RELIGION, AS ONE OF THE CORNERSTONES of the old order, was to be exterminated. No doubt of this had ever existed in the minds of the new rulers of Russia. But what were the best means to achieve this end? There were two factions within the ranks of the victors:

One believed that religion would crumble away of itself when it had been deprived of the State's political support and the bourgeoisie's economic support. This was the logical conclusion to be drawn from the Marxist interpretation of the role of religion in capitalist society. Religion was merely an instrument used by the oppressors of the people; liberated from the bonds of capitalism, people would understand that religion was their enemy and would rid their minds of religious superstition. Further, an overt attack on religion might revive the decaying fabric of the Church and make it a formidable enemy; they pointed out the errors of the French Revolution which they had studied thoroughly and which, they thought, collapsed mainly because of its rash assault on religion. The logical procedure was to separate religion from the State and to undermine its material existence, but not to go much further.

This program was opposed by the other faction whose

representatives thought that the victory of Communism was not yet final. The bourgeoisie was beaten, they said, but not totally annihilated; it certainly had not lost hope of avenging itself and would be likely to exploit the political inexperience of the workers. In so doing, it would naturally resort to religion. Therefore religion must not be left unmolested, but was to be fought with all the impetus of the newly acquired political power, and destroyed as quickly as possible. This demanded a violent intervention in the struggle between the old and the new faiths, an active anti-religious policy. But even the members of this second faction recognized the need of caution, since the effects of too drastic measures were unpredictable.

It is noteworthy that anti-religious strategy was one of the few questions to be debated during the elaboration of the new State's first Constitution. In the Constitutional Committee the relatively moderate members prevailed and consequently the Committee introduced into its draft the famous formula: "religion is a private affair of the citizens." But Lenin declared that this was not acceptable and ordered it to be replaced by another clause which guaranteed the freedom of religious and anti-religious propaganda.[1] This became Article 13 of the Constitution of the Russian Socialist Federal Soviet Republic of July 10, 1918, the archetype of all later Soviet constitutions.

The new clause seemed to be fairly moderate, for it apparently equalized religious and anti-religious propaganda. The actuality was different: religious propaganda was left to a weak Church, severely afflicted by the sudden destruction of its privileges, and anti-religious propaganda was to be furthered by the new State with the strong Communist party as its backbone. Actually, the formula in the new Constitution was a declaration of war on religion.

The assault had started before the enactment of the Constitution, and was only a consequence of the general antagonism described in Chapter One. Since in the inevitable struggle between Religion and Communism the active part was played by Communism, the struggle took on the sinister aspect of a religious persecution.

But has there ever been religious persecution under Communist rulers? Official spokesmen of the government emphatically deny it,[2] and many times their statements have been endorsed by pro-Communist writers. Moreover, in February, 1930, during one of the most all-out attacks on religion, Acting Patriarch Sergius told a group of amazed foreign correspondents that there was no religious persecution in Russia.[3] The official theory is that the Communist government had to prevent and repress rebellion wherever it found it, and that clergymen of various denominations were imprisoned, exiled, or executed not as clergymen, but as dangerous counter-revolutionaries; some churches have been closed; but, according to the official theory, this was spontaneously done by the masses forsaking religion, and without any official pressure.

The fallacy in such statements is obvious. That the government attacked religion against popular wishes, was many times conceded by the government itself;[4] and that not counter-revolution, but religion was the reason, is obvious from the fact that Roman Catholics were persecuted as fiercely as Greek Orthodox, although the former had no reason to desire a restoration of the *status quo ante*.[5]

There has been religious persecution, atrocious and reckless persecution. But it would be wrong to assume that, once started, the persecution followed one specified pattern. On the contrary, there have been many changes in methods and intensity; these were due to the desire of the Communist government to find increasingly efficient methods and to the necessity for adjusting anti-religious policy to changing conditions partly within the country, but mainly in the sphere of international relations. Consequently, there have been many fluctuations in the anti-religious tactics, and these may be understood only if they are studied period by period.

### 2

During the first period which lasted for more than four years (November, 1917–February, 1922), the anti-religious policy had three features.

The first feature was to deprive Churches of material means and legal existence. According to the sweeping decree of January 23, 1918, on the Separation of State and Church and of Church and School, all property owned by the Churches was "nationalized," *i.e.*, forfeited to the government without compensation.[6] The local Soviets could permit members of religious denominations to use so much of the nationalized property as was absolutely necessary for the performance of their rites: church buildings, chalices, vestments, etc. For this purpose, a contract was to be drawn up and signed by the Soviet and at least twenty believers. Certainly this permitted the continuance of divine service, but under conditions of incredible hardship. Not only did the Churches lose all they had accumulated; they were prevented from acquiring anything new. "No church or religious society has the right to own private property; such societies do not enjoy the rights of a juridical person," appeared in Article 12 of the decree. It is easy to understand the difficulties in organizing a material base for Church life, when neither the parishes nor dioceses nor national Churches might possess anything. All Church property became the property of individuals acting as trustees of the Church.[7]

On signing a contract, the religious group was not given exclusive possession of its building: ignoring the significance of the Consecration, the Commissariat of Justice [8] decided that a group could not object to its church being used for secular activities, such as courses of instruction, lessons, lectures, concerts, movies, discussions, meetings, and even popular dances.[9]

Moreover, weak and unorganized religious groups (so the parishes were officially designated) were all that legally remained of a formerly complicated and august Church administration. The decrees of 1918 did not recognize any religious organization except these groups; the Commissariat interpreted silence in the most unfavorable manner and directed the local administrative boards to close the diocesan consistories.

One of the corollaries drawn from the general non-recognition of religious organizations outside of the religious groups was the "liquidation" of monasteries. To prevent liquidation, some of them reorganized themselves into Labor Communes in accordance with the new legislation in favor of collective farming. The Commissariat of Justice inhibited this movement by ordering the Communes to accept, regardless of denomination, any person who might apply for membership. But usually volunteers did not show up, and the Communes into which old monasteries had been transformed frequently prospered because of their members' strict discipline. Cases have been reported where special commissions investigating such Communes found their economic status excellent through the improvement of agricultural techniques and the carrying on of all work without hired labor. Nevertheless, such Communes were dissolved whenever it was proved that they were ruled by their former monastic superiors, and finally it was decided to debar all former monks and nuns. This was a death sentence.

The second feature in the program for the first period had to do with reducing priests and other ministers to a status of social inferiority. Article 65 of the Constitution of 1918 proclaimed them to be non-workers and servants of the bourgeoisie, and together with the latter they were deprived of the franchise. No one cared to take part in Soviet elections, since the results were always known in advance; but disenfranchisement was a symbol for the deprivation of innumerable essential rights. In direct contrast with the promise of equality which had been so much stressed in Communist propaganda, Communist society became a caste society, and the disenfranchised formed within it the lowest caste. When ration cards were distributed, members of this caste, as a rule, received no cards at all or cards of the lowest category. They were not allowed to belong to the trade unions, to whose members appointment to State boards and enterprises was restricted. Since gradually everything was nationalized in the Soviet State, the clergy was prevented from earning money to supplement the meager donations of its parishioners. It had to pay higher rents for living quarters, and high income and agricultural taxes. Its children were deprived of the right to be educated in secondary schools and universities.

Officially, social inferiority was not extended to cover active laymen. However, in individual cases, belonging to religious fraternities was a stigma, almost as ominous as membership in any pre-revolutionary political party except the Bolshevik.

The third feature of the program involved destroying the Church's influence on various phases of life, especially on education.—Religious instruction was prohibited in State, public, and private schools by Article 9 of the decree of 1918. On June 13, 1921, it was forbidden to give religious instruction to organized groups of persons below the age of 18. Religious education could be given adults nowhere but in seminaries, where nothing but theology was taught; such schools were opened only by special permission of the provincial administration, and permits were not easily obtainable.

The spirit in which these regulations were applied clearly appears in a reply from the Commissariat of Justice of the Karelian autonomous territory to an application made by a township to have religious education restored in its schools. "The idea that man can fulfil his high destiny only on the basis of the Gospel is erroneous. It is obvious that religious education results in stupidity. As the Soviet Government is responsible for the children of the country, it must prevent the minds of these children from being darkened by religious superstition." [10]

The family was also "liberated" from Church influence. A decree of December 18, 1917, later incorporated in the Family Code of October 22, 1918, refused Church marriages and divorces legal recognition.[11] Only marriages and divorces performed by special State boards were recognized as valid. The new regulations made marriage rather a precarious union, to be dissolved whenever one of the parties wished to be emancipated from its bonds. The last straw was "postcard divorce": if a man or a woman told the registration office of his or her desire to have the marriage dissolved, the divorce was immediately signed and the other party informed by a postcard.

### 3

Even during the first period of persecution, local authorities, encountering an unexpected resistance in the people, applied more drastic measures, such as executing, exiling, or imprisoning bishops and priests, closing churches by force, and desecrating articles of religious veneration.[12] However, these measures remained sporadic, and the central authorities continued to insist that an open attack on religion would be fruitless. In March, 1921, with the shift to the New Economic Policy, capitalist methods of production and exchange were partially restored. As a counterbalance, "the ideological front" was to be stepped up by a direct attack on all religion, but especially on the Greek Orthodox and the Roman Catholic Churches.[13]

A painful conflict was purposely brought on by the Communist government on February 26, 1922, on the issue of a decree which ordered all articles of gold, silver, and precious stones to be surrendered under the pretext of helping the famished population of eastern Russia. Patriarch Tikhon, head of the Russian Orthodox Church, replied with a message on February 28, 1922, in which he declared that it was impossible to give away sacred vessels. The government insisted and ordered their removal by force, despite the offers of believers to pay the full value. Often the parishioners resisted. Some 1400 bloody fights around the churches have been reported in the Soviet press.[14] The following example gives an idea of what happened all over Russia:

"The District Executive Committee of Shuya organized a special commission to deal with the requisition of ecclesiastical treasures. On Monday, March 13, 1922, after the mass was over, the commission came to the church. But the crowd met it with hostile shouts. Wishing to avoid a conflict, the commission decided to postpone its work until Wednesday and left the spot. As it was leaving, the crowd indulged in some swearing, and the members of the Commission received several kicks and blows. On Wednesday, a large crowd began to assemble in the Cathedral Square before the service. A detachment of mounted police was stoned as soon as it approached. The tocsin resounded from the belfry and lasted an hour and a half attracting an enormous crowd. A detachment of infantry with machine guns was ordered to the spot. The crowd met them by a gale of stones and revolver shots. Five soldiers were swept away by the crowd and severely injured. After the first volley in the air, the second was directed at the crowd. Four people were killed and ten seriously injured, and then the crowd dispersed. Many arrests were made in the evening, and the commission continued to work. About 120 pounds of silver were requisitioned." [15]

To break up resistance, many clergymen and laymen were brought to trial. Almost invariably the indictment read as follows: "By proclaiming the church valuables inviolable, the defendants incited the masses of the people to engage in civil war." The climax was reached in the trial of "the fifty-four" in Moscow which included twenty high clergymen of the Orthodox Church, Metropolitan Benjamin in Petrograd, and a group of Roman Catholics headed by Bishop Jan Cepliak and Mgr. Budkiewicz. Twelve men in the first case, eleven in the second (including the Metropolitan) and two in the third (the Bishop and Mgr. Budkiewicz) were sentenced to death, and in most cases the sentence was carried out.[16]

The trial of the fifty-four caused an even greater sensation when Patriarch Tikhon was called as a witness. He firmly stated that he found himself compelled, in accordance with canon law, to condemn the confiscation of sacred vessels and that, in the event of a divergence between civil and canon law, he considered it his duty to obey the latter. On the basis of this declaration, the court ordered the Patriarch to be tried at once.

Ten months later, equally unflinching declarations were made by Bishop Cepliak and his companions. They asserted that as the sacred vessels belonged not to them but to the Church, no surrender could take place without the Papal permission; and that they must continue to teach the Catechism to children because no positive law could supersede the natural law which commanded priests to enlighten children.

The trials and executions were an attempt to intimidate the Churches and break their resistance. To destroy the Greek Orthodox Church, an additional instrument was used: that of fostering a schism. The opportunity occurred when some "progressive" priests who could not stomach the policy of Patriarch Tikhon met in council (May 12, 1922), declared the Patriarch unfit for further duty, announced the creation of a new religious organization called "The Living Church," expressed their hope of an agreement with the government, and outlined plans for far-reaching reforms, "before which Luther's reform would appear as child's play." [17] The government, departing from its former attitude of equal hostility to all religious groups, seized upon this welcome opening. The Patriarch was arrested; many church buildings were forcibly turned over to the Living Church; eighty-four bishops were expelled from their sees and more than a thousand priests from their parishes, to make room for the new organization.[18] As the result of the decision of the Communist government to interfere in intra-Church dissent, the Living Church for a while became the official Church of the Atheist State! In order to give this Church legal standing, a joint decree of the Commissariats of Justice and the Interior, on April 27, 1923, allowed all religious organizations to call provincial and central conventions and to elect executive boards, but only by special permission of the Soviet authorities. Of course such permissions were given only to the groups which had been persecuted under the old regime (the so-called sects) and to the Living Church. On the basis of these permissions diocesan and central boards of the Living Church were established whilst the old policy of non-recognition of central bodies was maintained toward the Orthodox Church.

However, disappointments were in store for the promoters of the Living Church and members of the Communist government who anticipated miraculous results from nursing dissent in the camp of the enemy. They reckoned without the laity, and the laity refused to follow the initiative of a few schismatic clergymen. So this Church, equipped with buildings, clergymen and power, had no flock. In many places, the laymen displayed their disgust in outright hostilities. Thus, in Petrograd, a leader of the Living Church, Archpriest Vvedensky, was struck by a stone; other members of the new Church were saved from similar experiences by the intervention of the Soviet police. Bishops and priests could not perform Divine Service or even appear in the churches.[19] No one was interested in the proceedings and the resolutions of the Council of the Living Church which met in May, 1923. About the same time, personal rivalry between the leaders became acute and the new Church broke up into a number of factions which assumed orotund names such as "The Ancient Apostolic Church," "Church Regeneration," and so on, and mauled one another in a battle of words.

Such a Church, or more exactly, such Churches, could not serve the government strategy. There was no remedy: a bold government may prevent people from going to church, but no government can compel them to attend a church which they dislike. The government had to reckon with the will of masses of Christians, and what had to happen, happened: the Living Church was dropped by the government. Quite unexpectedly for its leaders, on June 19, 1923, a decree was issued which prohibited local authorities from supporting certain religious groups against others. Reversing the policy of 1922–23, the Commissariat of Justice ordered the local authorities to distribute the church buildings under their jurisdiction among the existing religious groups, in proportion to the membership of these groups. However, complete equality was not restored, and for years the Patriarchal Church—this is the unofficial term used to designate that body of the Russian Church which was loyal to the Patriarch and his successors—remained suspect and oppressed, whereas the many branches of the Living Church were regarded with some benevolence, probably from a forlorn hope that they would finally be able to draw away the believers.

About this time the government made another forced retreat. Since May, 1922, the Patriarch had been in prison; his impending trial was announced and the indictment was of such a kind that he was threatened with execution. The turmoil and indignation in the country were enormous and no drastic measures could prevent clergy and laymen from expressing their devoted love to the imprisoned Patriarch. The movement spread abroad and a wave of indignation arose throughout Europe. Under the direct threat of the recall of the British mission [20] the Communists capitulated and released the Patriarch on June 27, 1923. Now the great danger was over. Conscious of the victory of the Patriarch and his increasing authority, most of the rebels among the clergy performed an act of subordination and were pardoned.[21] Until his death on April 7, 1925, the Patriarch enjoyed the love and veneration of his faithful sons.

### 4

The events of June, 1923, meant the breakdown of the first direct attack on religion. The Communist government had discovered from the application of persecution that Church authority was still vigorous. Consequently, election of a new Patriarch was prevented; successive Acting Patriarchs were imprisoned one after another, until in 1927 the last, Metropolitan Sergius of Nizhni Novgorod, was able to negotiate a compromise with the Communist government and thus retain his office. In a statement issued on August 19, 1927, he said: "I have taken upon myself, in the name of the whole of our Orthodox Church, hierarchy and flock, to register before the Soviet authorities our sincere readiness to be fully law abiding citizens of the Soviet Union, loyal to its government, and definitely to hold ourselves aloof from all political parties or enterprises seeking to harm the Union." The intention certainly was to make impossible any further identification between the Church and "counter-revolution." As later events proved, this declaration did not prevent the Communist government from badgering religion when it considered it expedient; on the other hand, the wording of the declaration appeared flabby and compromising to some of the Orthodox.

If, after 1923, the direct attack on the clergy and loyal laymen was discontinued and granting privileges to dissenters almost abandoned, new and more efficient methods were still looked for. The most important was systematically to calumniate the Church with mockeries and insults and to set up in opposition to religious faith a corpus of ideas based on materialistic atheism. To achieve this, in February, 1922, a "non-party publishing company" called "The Atheist" was formed.[22] An anti-religious seminary was opened in Moscow in November. On Christmas the first organized Anti-Christmas carnival was celebrated. It was described in the official paper of the Soviets as follows:

"Within ten days, forty preliminary meetings were organized, and the following themes were selected for the mock procession: the performance of miracles; opening holy shrines; the Immaculate Conception. The students of the Sverdlov University imitated the representatives of different religions. The rabbi and the archdeacon looked really genuine. To the tune of the Krakoviak (a lively Polish dance) the members of the Young Communist League danced around the procession." [23]

The papers noted that "anti-religious work which used to be of more or less casual character, was becoming one of the main branches of the Communist propaganda." [24] In order to organize the new activity, on February 7, 1925, a new body was formed which played an important role through the years that followed. This was the Militant Atheists League. Its beginning was modest: in 1928, three years after its creation, the League numbered only 123,000 members. However, from 1926 on, anti-religious propaganda of the most violent character was systematically disseminated by it. All means, including music halls, playing-cards and the children's ABC's, were pressed into service. Three lines of attack were chosen: first, a demonstration that religion, in all its forms, has always been the enemy of the workers; second, that natural science explained "everything" and left no room for religion; and third, that religious belief was a species of disloyalty to the Soviet State, for religion was incompatible with socialism.[25] The tone of this propaganda was grossly blasphemous and crudely insulting. God, Christ, the Virgin, and the Saints, to say nothing of bishops and priests, were shown in cartoons. All the ignoble lies about Christianity invented long ago by the first pagans, and all the subtle arguments propounded by the atheist philosophers of the eighteenth century, were repeated in a scandalous form which would, no doubt, have disgusted their comparatively civilized originators.[26]

Quality was not equal to quantity. Propaganda "was for the most part beneath criticism and never found a way that led to any solid success. The arguments put forward did not deserve any." They were such nonsense as "Holy Communion encourages drunkenness," [27] or that the airmen's "evidence" proves that "there are no gods because they had been up in the sky and could not find them." [28]

Anti-religious carnivals and other performances already in practice became one of the League's main functions. Year after year, Soviet papers repeated the information that, on Christmas Eve and on Holy Saturday, simultaneously with the beginning of divine service in the churches, various processions and demonstrations under the auspices of the League would begin, and last up to the end of the services.

Meanwhile, the methods inaugurated before the direct attack of 1922–23 were not forgotten and, when possible, renewed and resharpened.[29] Although church buildings were, as previously, placed at the disposal of religious groups free of charge, the land on which the churches were built was taxable; this had been the case since 1917, but now taxes went higher and higher. The church buildings had to be insured, and the religious groups must pay for this; in December, 1923, it was decided that, if the building were destroyed by fire, the sums paid to the insurance board nevertheless would become State property, as the church building had been. The fact that premiums had been paid by the believers was disregarded, and a fire could actually serve two purposes: to destroy a church and to help the government to make money! Teaching religion in churches was forbidden on July 16, 1924, and on September 1, teaching religion privately to groups of more than three children was prohibited. On July 30, 1923, official holidays which, up to that date, had coincided with Church holidays, were transferred to the so-called "New Calendar," [30] so that Church holidays became working days and could no longer be appropriately celebrated. It is noteworthy that Patriarch Tikhon made an attempt to meet the situation by shifting the Church holidays to the New Calendar, in other words by accepting the Calendar of the Western Church; but, in this case, he was not followed by the believers who, having in mind the plans of the Living Church, fearing any change and especially not wanting alterations sponsored by the Communist government,[31] insisted on adhering to the old calendar. The Patriarch reconsidered his order, and the change in the Church calendar was discontinued.

An additional hardship had been imposed on the Church by the decree of December 26, 1922, obliging the priests to submit their sermons to the censor. In the preamble to the decree, religion was declared to be "a brutalization of the people," and it was stated that "education was to be so directed so as to efface from the people's mind this humiliation and this idiocy."

Toward the end of this period, measures were taken to discredit all vestiges of the "Orthodox Way of Life": in 1928, the sale of Easter food and Christmas trees was prohibited, and no festoons of Christmas ornaments were displayed in shop windows; they were replaced by mountains of special "anti-Christmas literature." [32]

5

In 1929, the failure of all the methods to destroy religion
used in 1923–28 was so obvious that the government inaugurated a new plan. This plan combined a renewal of the
direct attack, an entirely new scheme which might be called
"cultural strangulation," and the introduction of strictly
anti-religious education in schools.

This time, direct attack took the form of mass closures,
on the pretext that Russia was being transformed into a socialist society, and that members of a socialist society could
not want churches. "In thousands of villages where wholesale collectivization of farming was going on, local Communists or members of the Young Communists League
called meetings which voted over the heads of the congregations to demolish the churches, melt down the bells, or
turn church buildings into granaries, schools, movie theaters.
. . . A semblance of popular consent was thus created. But
when brigades arrived to remove the bells and icons, they
sometimes found believers armed with sticks and pitchforks,
to defend their church. The troops in many instances were
summoned to crush these riots and the ringleaders found
themselves quickly enough in prison or before the firing
squad."[33] In this manner, 1440 churches were closed during the year 1929.[34]

Some incidents in the last months of 1929 and the first
months of 1930 may illustrate the variety of the seizures.
Thus, in the Khoper district together with the rapid collectivization of homesteads, local authorities closed all
churches; the same thing happened in the Novgorod district. In the province of Ivanovo, twenty churches were

closed during a few days. In the provinces of Riazan and Tambov, a traveling anti-religious movie theater showed motion pictures in church buildings; then, usually, after the performance, a resolution was passed by the audience to close the church or to secularize it. The item on this traveling theater mentions that, in some place, the "kulaks" (rich peasants) organized resistance, but that, without exception, their resistance was overcome. In Archangel, the town soviet prohibited the ringing of bells, and this practice was imitated in many other towns. In Samara (now Kuibysheff) the Soviet ordered all bells to be taken down. In Tver (now Kalinin) the Soviet forbade the churches to be lighted by electricity. In Briansk, the closing of all churches was decided upon at a meeting of workmen and a resolution passed which demanded the closure of all the churches in the State.[35]

The mass closure of the churches was accompanied by a comprehensive attack on the personnel of the Church. In many dioceses bishops were arrested, as they had been in 1922–23; when successors were appointed, they were arrested in their turn. Most often, they were transported to the famous concentration camp set up in the former Solovetski monastery, on a group of islands in the White Sea.[36] One time there were about 150 bishops rounded up, more than the number of dioceses in the Russian Church. In this way the atheist government planned to destroy the vital Apostolic succession.

Many priests shared the fate of their superiors. They were exiled or executed in thousands as participants in the covert civil war which accompanied the collectivization of farming. The priests were innocent of rebellion. But, in many places, the peasantry killed especially hated rural officials, and the Communist practice was to seize on every opportunity to rid themselves of the undesirable. So, in retaliation, they executed not only murderers, nor only those who could be plausibly represented as agitators, but also those whose very existence impeded the execution of state policy, and priests often fell into the last category. Time and again, hostages were taken and, naturally, priests were first chosen.[37]

A decree of December 27, 1932, brought new hardships to priests who were not yet imprisoned. It introduced a passport system and prohibited all "non-workers" from residing in big cities and their environs. Consequently, priests could no longer live in cities and had to come from the country to do their work. "They had often found homes among the peasantry, but the peasants who harbored them were more heavily taxed." [38]

Another act was closely connected with the direct attack. A six-day week was introduced by a decree of September 24, 1929, making it difficult for workers to attend church on Sundays, unless Sunday happened to coincide with the sixth or rest day of the new week. After the enactment of the law of November 20, 1932, according to which failure to appear for a single working day became a legitimate reason for dismissal, church attendance, except on the rest day, became practically impossible.

Cultural strangulation, the second and most important element in the new plan, was the atheist government's reaction to an unexpected development of Church life: since 1917, but especially in the later twenties, the Church had become a center of cultural and social activities.[39] To root up this new development, a decree was issued on April 8,

1929.[40] *It embodied all earlier regulations of Church affairs and therefore might be called the second sweeping decree.*[41] It also imposed new restrictions on religious societies, especially on their cultural and social activities. Article 17 forbade religious societies to form mutual aid associations, cooperatives, and, in general, to make use of their property [42] for any purpose except the offering of worship; to give material aid to their members; to organize special prayer or Bible classes or other meetings for children, adolescents and women; to organize groups, circles, or excursions; to open playgrounds, libraries, reading rooms; to operate sanitariums and to offer medical aid. This long catalogue of forbidden activities clearly shows how manifold the functions of the Church had become. Now, in the words of an official spokesman, "the activities of all religious associations were reduced to the performance of the cult. Activities exceeding the limits whereby this need was satisfied were no longer permitted." [43]

The new regulation meant, among other things, that the Church was refused the right of circulating religious propaganda which had been explicitly recognized by the Constitution of July 10, 1918 (literally reproduced as far as religion was concerned by the new version of May 11, 1925). To make things final, a constitutional amendment was adopted on May 22, 1929. Whereas the older Constitutions had proclaimed the liberty of religious and anti-religious propaganda, now "freedom of religious worship and of anti-religious propaganda" was declared. According to an authoritative interpretation, the new text of the Constitution no longer permitted either "the winning of new groups of toilers, especially of children, as adherents of religion," or "any kind of propaganda on the part of the churches and religious persons." [44] In other words, says a foreign observer, "no church representative, no individual believer was any longer permitted to reply in speech or writing to the attacks on religion in the numerous anti-religious publications." [45]

Other restrictions of organizational activity were imposed by the new decree. Only those members of a denomination who resided in one city and vicinity, or in one village, or in several villages of the same township, could form a religious association; this was directed against denominations whose parishioners were widely spread out, in particular the Roman Catholics. A religious association was permitted to use only one church building; this was directed against large parishes which had survived the persecutions of previous years and possessed chapels in addition to a main church. The religious organizations were explicitly forbidden to organize any collections: donations had to be absolutely spontaneous.

Additional pressure was brought to bear on religion through the trade unions which were completely under the thumb of the Communist government. At a conference of the Militant Atheists League held June 10–13, 1929, the representatives of the Young Communist League ntroduced a motion to compel trade unionists (in practice, all workers, civil officers and professional men) to withdraw from membership in religious associations. The majority, led by Lunacharsky, the Commissar of Education, refused to follow suit, explaining that such measures would merely intensify the religious sentiment. However, under another guise, the cooperation of the trade unions was won by the Militant Atheists League. In the Fall of 1929, locals of the trade union of printers, directed by the Central Committee of the Printers Union, refused to print religious work. Locals of the transport workers refused to transport works or articles intended for religious ceremonies. Locals of the Union of Post and Telegraph workers stopped answering calls to or from members of the clergy. This meant social isolation, another form of the cultural strangulation.[46]

A third approach of the new plan was the extension of social inferiority to all active lay members of the Churches. This part of the plan was not openly promulgated in any law or decree; but the study of Soviet papers shows that for years no opportunity was given faithful Christians to advance either in the administration or in professional careers or even in industry.[47] The following statements from the report of an American professor who spent six weeks in Russia in the summer of 1935 are illuminating:

"A woman of the intelligentsia told the reporter that she herself was a Christian and that she could not admit it publicly and keep her job with the government. Another woman, a fellow passenger on a Volga boat, congratulated the foreigner on his wearing a wedding ring. She herself was the wife of a University Professor; her mother, dying some two years previous, asked to have a religious burial. When this woman insisted upon fulfilling her mother's wish, she was discharged from her position and since has been unable to find work. A prominent physician said that he had recently finished a long prison sentence for his refusal to sign an antireligious document. He was released from prison but never restored to his position in a government hospital." [48]

Finally, whereas up till now the teaching in schools was

non-religious, i.e., free from any reference to God or religion, during this period, teaching became actively anti-religious. The change was announced by Lunacharsky at the same session of the Congress of Soviets which voted the previously mentioned constitutional reform. In an article published a little earlier, he explained that "a believing teacher in a Soviet school was an awkward contradiction" and that "the departments of popular education were bound to use every opportunity to replace such teachers with new ones, of anti-religious sentiment." [49]

Accordingly, textbooks were introduced in schools which taught the class roots of religion and its incompatibility with science. Sociology based upon the materialism and atheism of Marx and Lenin became one of the most important subjects in the school curriculum. Excursions to anti-religious museums, special anti-religious conferences and discussions, and anti-religious readings supplemented the instruction of the Soviet teacher. How the new program was carried out may be seen from the following eye-witness report:

"After a lecture to young children on Roman history which I heard admirably delivered, the teacher at the end stopped and, *apropos* of nothing, added: 'And who was it who broke the yoke of religion? Charles Darwin, an Englishman.' Later on she mentioned apologetically that it was the end of the term and that the anti-religious idea had to be introduced somewhere." [50]

Naturally the Militant Atheists League made tremendous advances during these years of the systematic attack. In 1932, the membership reached five and a half million, and grandiose plans for having fifteen million five years later were set forth. A five-year plan was discussed by the League which looked to the utter extermination of religion.[51]

However, the direct attack proposed by the new plan once more proved to be a failure. The peasants resisted collectivization not only because they did not want to lose their economic freedom, but also because it was combined with the closing of their churches. Their resistance was a refusal to work, and it was feared that there would be almost no harvest in the Fall of 1930. The government recognized the danger and decided to separate collectivization and the dechristianization of the countryside. A decree which was issued on March 15, 1930, acknowledged that the closing of the churches was effected by local authorities against the will of the people and ordered the cessation of the measure. A few weeks later, Yaroslavsky, the head of the Militant Atheists League, published an article in which he ridiculed those who prepared masquerades for the Easter night or elaborated plans for mass demonstrations, or organized an orchestra or dancing party in order to divert people from going to church [52]—a clear-cut case of the usual hypocrisy of the Communist leaders who shift the responsibility for their failures onto the shoulders of drudges who have faithfully followed out directions.

Very likely another factor had some influence on the decision of the government to call off the direct attack. A severe condemnation by Pope Pius XI and the Christian Protest Movement which, about that time, had gained momentum in England, threatened the Soviet rulers with the withdrawal of recognition by many States. This menace was felt by them because they urgently needed foreign help for the realization of the first Five-Year Plan.

6

An important part of the plan of 1929–30 was consequently dropped. But other aspects, especially cultural
strangulation, were systematically carried out up to the years
1934–35. Then began a new period characterized by a number of small concessions on the part of the government not
made because of a changed attitude toward religion, but as
a part of a general policy of concessions and adjustments to
the feelings and desires of the people, a policy which cannot
be explained except by the unfavorable change in the international situation.[53]

Anti-Easter and anti-Christmas carnivals were gradually
stopped. On an unknown day they were forbidden by central authority. When, at Christmas, 1935, they took place
in Ekaterinburg (now Sverdlovsk) and Vologda, the insti-
gators were officially censored.[54] According to some reports,
on Easter, 1936, Soviet policemen no longer "tolerated hoo-
ligans, whether against the godly or godless." [55] When, in
April, 1937, a mass campaign for the closing of churches
was started in the province of Vologda, the provincial committee of the Militant Atheists League, directed from above,
explained that such a campaign was not permissible, for it
could only embitter the believers, and could not help to rid
them of religion.[56]

At Easter, 1935, sale in the markets of special ingredi-
ents needed for the traditional Easter cakes and meats was
once more authorized; later these goods could be bought
even in State stores (stores of the atheist State), and this
despite their connection with the "Orthodox way of life."
At Christmas in 1935, the population was once more al-

lowed to light Christmas trees, an act which had been strictly
forbidden for many years. Ostensibly the permissions were
granted for New Year's celebrations, but Christmas comes
in Russia on January 7,[57] and it is reported that the New
Year tree, in many instances, was hidden indoors until then.

In November, 1936, an almost incredible episode got
wide publicity. A new version of Borodin's opera "Bogatyri"
(The Knights) was produced by the famous Kamerny
Theater (headed by Tairov), with a libretto by Demyan
Byedny, the official poet of the new regime. But after a few
performances the opera was suppressed by the Central Arts
Committee because a scene in the new version ridiculed the
Christianization of Russia by Prince Vladimir by burlesquing
mass baptism as a drunken farce. The Committee issued the
following statement:

"It is well known that the Christianization of Russia was
one of the principal factors in the rapprochement of the
backward Russian people with the people of Byzantium and
later with the peoples of the West, namely with peoples of
higher culture. It is also well known what a big part clergymen, particularly Greek clergymen, played in promoting
literacy in the Russia of the Kiev period; thus from a historical standpoint Byedny's libretto is an example not only
of an anti-Marxist, but also of a frivolous attitude towards
history and a cheapening of the history of our people." [58]

In the course of the same month, it was reported that "the
Soviet State has begun manufacturing wedding rings. They
are on sale at the Central Mostorg. . . . Thus an ancient
symbol of bourgeois (religious) marriage has emerged . . .
from the bootlegger stage; even though in nearly all cases
the purchase of wedding rings means that a Soviet couple

intends to reinforce the simple registration at the bureau with a religious ceremony." [59]

This was only a final episode in an important development which had begun much earlier. In the Summer of 1934, the Communist government discontinued its efforts to loosen family ties. Frequent divorces and remarriages were described as "a petty bourgeois deviation from Communist ideals"; a few measures were taken to make divorce a little more difficult, such as increasing fees and requiring the registration of marriages and divorces on passports, so that "silly girls would think it over twice before marrying a man with twenty or thirty marriage records"; among other things, the "postcard divorce" was abolished.[60] Religious arguments, of course, were not used, but obviously this gesture was welcomed by all Christian people and organizations.

Not directly related to religion, but nevertheless extremely important in improving its general status were the following events: On April 24, 1934, a "resolution" of the Central Committee of the Communist Party acknowledged that indoctrination with official dogma was considered a bore by all students of Soviet schools and diverted them from social activities. Consequently, teaching the theory of Marx and Lenin was discontinued in grammar schools and substantially restricted in high schools, but was left almost intact in institutions for higher education.

On December 29, 1935, a decree abolished discrimination against the children of non-workers entering schools, and sons and daughters of the clergy were allowed to enroll in all grades. There was some resistance on the part of the local authorities who, as usual, did not realize the magnitude of the new tack. A test case was selected for discussion; it had to do with a priest's daughter from the North Caucasus whose right to study was denied by local authorities, but emphatically recognized by the center. Finally, the new Constitution of December 5, 1936, abolished the disenfranchisement of priests and all other "non-workers." [61]

## 7

The lull in persecution did not last. In August, 1937,[62] there was a sudden reversal of the current and a third outburst was launched. This followed the enactment of the new Constitution which was proclaimed the most democratic in the world. The first purpose of the attack was to prevent religious organizations from having any influence on the elections to the Supreme Soviet which were to be held in the course of the months of November and December. The leaders of the Churches were once more castigated as implacable enemies of social reconstruction, whereas the rank and file of the laity were assumed to be honest and loyal members of the socialist society: a significant departure from previous methods.[63] This third attack coincided with the climax of the terror directed by Yezhoff, the Commissar of the Interior.[64]

Both foreign correspondents and Soviet papers gave ample information on the subject. "A new fight against religion has begun in the Soviet Union," was stated in October. "The clergy is accused of insidious propaganda for the revival of the sorely oppressed Church. Their aim is the election of friendly deputies in the Soviets. Trade Unions have been expected to revive the fight against religion and to expose the machinations of priests and believers." [65]

In November, 1937, groups of churchmen, including bishops, were arrested all over the Soviet Union on charges of organizing espionage and sabotage in the interest of Germany and Japan and even in one case of plotting the assassination of Soviet leaders. Their alleged crimes included the firing of a village school which resulted in the death of twenty children after failing in their efforts to hinder the collectivization of agriculture. Bishop D. of Moscow was accused of collecting 200,000 rubles from communicants to organize espionage for the German Gestapo. Bishop Z. of Voronezh was accused of writing a treatise blessing terrorism as a legitimate mode of Church opposition to Soviet power and declaring it to be a Christian duty to take up arms.[66] The arrests made public in November were "only the latest in a series of trials of various religious groups for anti-Soviet activity. One of the largest of these was the trial of thirty religionists, including a bishop, several priests and nuns, former landlords and one former duke from Orel. The beginning of the trial was reported in the organ of the Militant Atheists, but its end has never been disclosed." [67]

The charges against clergymen were similar to those made about the same time in the trials against the Old Guard of the Communist Party (Kamenev, Zinovyev, Bukharin, and others) and of the leaders of the Red Army (Tukhachevsky and others). They were as incredible as the charges made against the latter, and the reason for using them was the same: The Communist government wanted to profit from the rising patriotism of the population and hoped, by associating the Church with the enemies of Russia, finally to destroy its prestige.

Once launched, the attack continued after the elections

were over. In 1938, "the Russian Easter was marked by the announcement of wholesale arrests of religious people. The prisoners included one archbishop, one bishop, one former count who had been a large landlord, six priests, six monks, two nuns, a former merchant, a former 'kulak,' and so on. The charges ranged from espionage in the interests of foreign States to the setting up of a 'miracle factory' in Moscow. The archbishop was charged with instructing his followers to organize secret churches in their homes and set up secret monasteries. The charges went on to assert that the leaders (namely the archbishop, the bishop and the count) were connected with secret fascist services and carried on an active struggle against the Soviet regime with the object of having trained personnel among the clergy for aggressive activities when the capitalist countries should declare war on the Soviet Union." [68]

All through this period Soviet papers were full of reports about "concrete hostile acts" committed by religionists, such as setting fire to a factory, or causing accidents in coal mines. These charges are as hard to believe as those mentioned above. It is significant that during this time, in distinction to what happened during the earlier periods of direct attack, unmistakably religious activities were also punished. Thus, for instance, in Petrograd (Leningrad), the Metropolitan Joseph and two priests were "liquidated" for having given assistance to travelling priests. [69] In the same city, authorities hunted down followers of the late Father John of Cronstadt. [70] In the province of Petrograd, seven young peasants were tried for having gathered together to read the Bible aloud. One of them was sentenced to ten years in prison, another to eight. In Tsaritsyn (Stalingrad) authorities searched for followers of the monk Iliodor.[71] The bishop of this city was tried for having explained the Holy Writ to children who came to see him. A wholesale "liquidation" of clergy was reported in the Crimea. There priests were accused of stealing church property and of immoral conduct. In the Khakas autonomous district (Siberia) members of the Sabbath sect were arrested and tried for reading the Bible aloud, and for refusing to desist from the celebration of Christian and Hebrew holidays.[72]

A number of trifling measures were introduced to combat the renascence of religious life.[73] Thus, the Party elaborated techniques against mass baptism. If a travelling priest succeeded in baptizing school children, not only the priest was to be tried, but also the local teachers and the representatives of the Young Communist League as accessories in "gross deception of people." In the Donets region, those desiring to join the Stakhanov movement were required by the local authorities to present a written promise to enlist in the fight against religion. Pioneers were instructed to ridicule school children who wore crosses or prayed to God.[74]

At the same time, during this severe persecution, certain phases of the previous more lenient policy were preserved. Thus, direct interference with public worship by anti-religious manifestations was still forbidden; campaigns for the closing of churches were suppressed; the rehabilitation of many of the national heroes, despite their affiliation with religion, continued.[75] However, by arresting priests and heavily taxing religious associations,[76] the government succeeded in substantially decreasing the number of open churches. During the year 1937, 1100 Orthodox churches, 240 Catholic churches, 61 Protestant prayer houses and 110 mosques were closed.[77] Figures for 1938 are lacking, but the total decrease in the number of religious associations, in the course of 1937–38, was about 10,000.[78]

The period of acute persecution ended as suddenly as it had begun. The change coincided with the dismissal of Yezhoff. It must not be thought that his successor, Beria, was a better or milder man; but new instructions were given him, and from January, 1939, on, a new era in the history of religious persecution is noticeable. We might speak of a "New Religious Policy," analogous to the "New Economic Policy" of the years 1929–39. This policy will be described in a special chapter (Five).

## FOOTNOTES TO CHAPTER TWO

(1) G. S. Gurvitch, *A History of the Soviet Constitution* (in Russian), Moscow, 1923, pp. 79–80.

(2) This formula was first invented by the Soviet government when Mgr. Budkiewicz was martyred and later was repeated by Krassin (the Soviet Ambassador in Great Britain) to newspaper interviewers and to members of the British Labor Party.

(3) The peculiar circumstances in which this declaration was made deprive it of any significance. W. H. Chamberlin (who was present when the declaration was made) gives the details in *Russia's Iron Age,* London, 1936, pp. 323–24.

(4) See chapter IV, section 1.

(5) In January, 1923, Bishop Cepliak wrote to the British representative in Petrograd: "Both the priests and the Catholic population have always been loyal to the Soviet government" (quoted by F. Mac-Cullagh, *The Bolshevik Persecution of Christianity*, N. Y., 1924, p. 114). At the trial he declared that the Revolution set the Catholics free and that the idea of counter-revolution did not enter the minds of the Catholics (*ibid.,* pp. 201 and 254).

(6) The decree was patterned on the well-known French laws of the years 1905–06. For a detailed study of this decree see: N. S. Timasheff "Staat und Kirche," in a symposium *Das Recht Sowjetrusslands,* Tübingen, 1925, and "The Church and the State in Soviet Russia," *Put* (in Russian), 1927 No. 10, and V. Gsovsky, "The Legal Status of

the Church in Soviet Russia," *Fordham Law Review*, 1939, pp. 1–28.

(7) Since private property was often confiscated, this regulation did not give any guarantee at all to the modest sums collected by the religious associations.

(8) Which, up to 1924, was in charge of the religious affairs of the atheist State. In France, after the enactment of the laws mentioned in note 6, religious problems usually were managed by the Ministry of Justice. The Communists probably imitated the French regulation.

(9) A complete compilation of laws, decrees, instructions, and circulars about religion, enacted up to 1926, is to be found in Gidulyanov, *The Separation of Church and State* (in Russian), 3rd edition, Moscow, 1926. This work has been amply used in the text.

(10) Gidulyanov, *op. cit.*, pp. 368–69.

(11) However, only those performed after the enactment of the decree.

(12) For a compilation of data concerning the unorganized persecutions of the years 1917-1923 see A. A. Valentinov, *The Assault of Heaven*, London, 1925, pp. 13–22. The number of victims is unknown. The Greek Orthodox Church venerates the memory of 28 bishops and more than one thousand priests as having died for Christ, up to 1923. 58 shrines with relics of saints were opened up to 1925 (Gidulyanov, *op. cit.*, p. 25).

(13) The most complete description of this attack, containing a detailed account of the trial of Bishop Cepliak and Msgr. Budkiewicz, has been given by MacCullagh, *op. cit.*

(14) P. 1922, No. 110.

(15) I. March 28, 1922.

(16) 45 executions and 250 long prison terms have been reported as the result of the trials. (J. F. Hecker, *Religion and Communism*, N. Y., 1930, p. 209.)

(17) Detailed accounts of the schism have been given by M. Spinka, *The Church and the Russian Revolution*, N. Y., 1927 (favorable to the reformers) and by W. C. Emhard, *Religion in Russia*, London, 1929 (favorable to the Patriarchal Church). *Cf.* also Miliukoff (see Selected Bibliography), pp. 164–191.

(18) MacCullagh, *op. cit.*, p. XVII.

(19) B. V. Titlinov, *The New Church* (in Russian), Petrograd, 1923, p. 51.

(20) MacCullagh, *op. cit.*, p. 71.

(21) The names of the bishops who returned to the Patriarch are given by Emhard, *op. cit.*, p. 320. The most significant of the acts of subordination, that of Metropolitan Sergius, later on the Acting Patriarch, is described as follows: "Publicly, on his knees before the Patriarch, dressed in the garb of a simple monk, he made an act of peni-

tence, and after this received anew, from the Patriarch, the *mitra"* (*ibid.*, p. 320).

(22) I. August 5, 1922; MacCullagh, *op. cit.*, p. 375.

(23) I. January 10, 1923.

(24) P. May 30, 1923.

(25) P. April 13, 1928; Chamberlin, *op. cit.*, p. 315.

(26) The best work on anti-religious propaganda has appeared in Italian; this is Lino Capuccio, *URSS regno dell'anticristo*, Milano, 1933.

(27) The Greek Orthodox Church administers Holy Communion to laymen in the two species.

(28) Sir Bernard Pares, *Russia*, Penguin Books, 1940, p. 172.

(29) Even methods belonging to the system of direct attack were not completely forgotten. Thus, for instance, in 1928 the Roman Catholic bishop Skalsky was sentenced to 10 years of prison for "counter-revolution and espionage." P. January 28, 1928.

(30) This is the name used in Russia for the calendar of the Western Church.

(31) The shift to the new calendar in civil life was ordered by the Communist government as of January 1, 1918.

(32) K.G. March 22, 1928; Chamberlin, *op. cit.*, p. 316.

(33) E. Lyons, *Assignment to Utopia*, New York, 1937, pp. 212–13.

(34) A. 1930, No. 3.

(35) N. S. Timasheff, "Religious Persecution in Russia," *Vozrozhdeniye* (published in Russian in Paris), January 14 and 18, 1930.

(36) This camp has been described by Professor V. Chernavin, *I Speak for the Silent*, London, 1935.

(37) Sometimes priests were arrested and imprisoned on charges of hoarding, because parish funds were naturally passing through their hands. Pares, *op. cit.*, p. 174.

(38) Pares, *op. cit.*, p. 174.

(39) *Cf.* below chapter III section I.

(40) For a complete study of this decree see Gsovsky, *op. cit.*, and N. S. Timasheff, "The Codification of Soviet Law on Religion," *Put* (in Russian), 1929, No. 17.

(41) The first one being that of January 23, 1918.

(42) According to law, churches could not own property; the decree obviously had to do with funds managed by the trustees.

(43) N. Orleansky, *The Law Concerning Religious Associations in the USSR* (in Russian), Moscow, 1930, p. 11. This work has superseded that of Gidulyanov (see note 9) in the quality of a semi-official commentary.

(44) *Ibid.*, p. 47.

(45) Chamberlin, *op. cit.*, p. 320.

(46) N. S. Timasheff, "Religious Persecution in Russia," quoted *supra,* in note 35.

(47) P., May 7, 1937, incidentally remarked that "our organizations dismiss people from their jobs under the pretext that they are believers." S. and B. Webb were extremely ill informed when they wrote: "There is no exclusion from offices of men who are believers" (*Soviet Communism,* London, 1935, p. 1010.)

(48) The reporter did not permit the disclosure of his identity.

(49) P. March 26, 1929.

(50) Pares, *op. cit.,* p. 174.

(51) A. 1930 No. 3.

(52) B. 1930 No. 17–18.

(53) *Cf.* below chapter VI, section 2.

(54) A. 1939 No. 1.

(55) *New York Herald Tribune,* April 13, 1936.

(56) A. 1938, No. 5.

(57) January the seventh corresponds to December 25th of the old calendar.

(58) *New York Times,* November 10, 1936.

(59) *Ibid.,* November 18, 1936.

(60) Very good accounts of the change in the Soviet attitude towards the family may be found in *Russie et Chrétienté* (published by the Dominican Center *Istina*), Paris, 1935, No. 3 and 5–6, 1936, No. 4.

(61) N. S. Timasheff, "The Soviet Constitution," *Thought,* Dec., 1941.

(62) Preparing the attack, since the beginning of the year 1937, central and local newspapers increased the number of anti-religious articles (Yaroslavsky, *Expand Antireligious Propaganda,* (in Russian), 1937, p. 3).

(63) A. 1938, No. 1.

(64) September 27, 1936–December 8, 1938.

(65) *Christian Science Monitor,* October 26, 1937.

(66) *New York Times,* November 23, 1937.

(67) *Ibid.*

(68) *New York Times,* April 25, 1938. In 1939, the anti-religious press mentioned that, in 1937, trials of "religionists" had taken place in the provinces of Nizhni Novgorod, Smolensk, Orel, Omsk, and "some others" (A. 1939, No. 10). However, no details were given.

(69) On the travelling priests see chapter III, section 3.

(70) Around 1900 Father John of Cronstadt was considered by many to be a man of holy life; his later canonization was expected.

(71) Monk Iliodor was a dubious personality who took part in intrigues around Rasputin; however, there were people who believed him to be a holy man.

(72) B. 1938, Nos. 17 and 24; and 1939, No. 2; T., April 24, 1936; K.G., October 27, 1938.

(73) About these forms see chapter III, section 3.

(74) T. 1938, No. 66; K.P., March 27, 1938. The Stakhanov movement, named after an obscure miner of the Donets basin, originated in August, 1935, and involved a large increase in the output of individual workers who were magnificently remunerated by the Communist government. Pioneers are members of an official organization preparing children to become members of the Young Communist League.

(75) See chapter V, sections 2 and 3.

(76) 145 million rubles in 1937, *versus* 89 million in 1936.

(77) Professor I. A. Ilyin, *Rossia* (published in Russian, in New York), September 25, 1941.

(78) See chapter III, section 2.

# CHAPTER THREE

# The Resistance of the Believers

I

THE FACT that religious persecution has never stopped in Russia since the inauguration of the Communist rule, and the fact that as late as 1937–38 an exceptionally energetic attack on religion was launched, are sufficient proof of the strong resistance of the believers; had they never resisted or had their resistance been broken after a few years, then the perseverance of the government in combating religion would be inexplicable.

Naturally the form and the intensity of the resistance have varied with the form and intensity of the persecution. During the early years, when the State harried the Churches by depriving them of material means and legal status, the parishioners retaliated by persistently gathering round the churches and by emphasizing their participation in religious activities.[1] Despite the wholesale expropriation of wealth throughout the country, the devout collected their meager resources to provide for their priests; if they could not give money (and money very soon became worthless as the result of inflation) they gave food or fuel. In the summer, pious men repaired church buildings; in the winter, men and women worked inside the churches, often in temperatures below freezing, cleaning and embellishing, assisting in the divine service as readers or singers in the choir; needless to say, they were not paid for their work.

Divine service became more frequent than ever before. Bishops visited their parishes more often and were greeted by large crowds. Holy icons, particularly those thought miraculous, were carried from church to church to permit everyone to worship them. A Eucharistic movement was begun and thousands of men and women pledged themselves to receive Holy Communion at least once a month. On church holidays, symbolic processions were organized, attracting tens of thousands in the big cities. Priests and laymen took part in discussions under the auspices of the promoters of the anti-religious campaign, and frequently "found their best support in the shrewd intelligence of the peasant." [2] Philosophical and religious groups conducted forums and discussions on metaphysical subjects, continuing the intellectual movement that had begun shortly before the Revolution.

The Greek Orthodox Church undertook tasks which had heretofore been the business of other agencies: it furthered religious education (this was not yet prohibited); it collected funds and food for the relief of the needy; fraternities and sisterhoods were formed in the parishes and contributed greatly to the religious revival.

To be sure, the revival was not universal. Those whose faith was superficial left the Church to seek favor in the eyes of the new rulers or simply cancelled their membership. But the faith of the true Christians was inflamed, and, moreover, many conversions of people who had been indifferent to religion were accomplished. Among the intellectuals, the feeling was especially strong, for to the majority of these the

Communist Revolution was a spiritual catastrophe: they had "believed" in the people almost as Christians believe in God, but the people had betrayed them and given power to the anti-intellectual Communist Party.[3] They saw that their devotion to the people had been a *vanitas vanitatum* and that the true solution lay in the return to God. These conversions greatly strengthened the Church, for many of the intellectuals became ordained priests, thereby elevating the standards of the clergy, and refreshing the cultural and social life of the Greek Orthodox Church.

The revival was not limited to the intellectuals. Contrary to the expectations of the Communists, many factory workers appeared to be or to become faithful sons of the Church, who, in many cases, frustrated the local authorities in their plans to demolish churches or to arrest or execute clergymen.

Toward the end of these early years, which had been characterized by a relatively mild anti-religious program, a kind of show-down took place in Petrograd. In 1921, Greek Orthodox Easter coincided with the Labor Day of the Soviet State, celebrated on May 1. A great labor demonstration was planned and, in order to prove the decay of religion in socialist society, the government sanctioned a religious procession on the following Sunday, in the hope that it would be ill-attended. However, the Labor Day demonstration was a complete failure because church members refused to take part in it, and on Sunday the Church was triumphant in its procession in which about two hundred thousand people walked. Almost all day, the streets of the former capital of Russia were crowded with people bearing crosses, church banners and other religious symbols, and singing religious songs. The reaction of the government was not apparent, but the blow was heavy and still smarted when circumstances moved the State to "actualize" its anti-religious policy.

This "actualization" was part of the New Economic Policy, inaugurated in March, 1921. Having partly restored economic freedom, the government feared that religion and the liberated economic forces might form a formidable coalition. Such fears were the result of Marxist reasoning rather than of any observation of facts: the behavior of priests and active laymen was not at all what it should have been according to the official doctrine, for they adhered more firmly than ever to the principle, "My realm is not of this world." When their spiritual life was threatened, they resisted, but their intention had never been to interfere in politics. Consequently, the persecution was mitigated when the leaders realized (1) that no political scheme was implicit in the continuance of faith and religious practices, (2) that a direct offensive rather strengthened than weakened the Churches, and (3) that the defensive was invincible and a continued onslaught might result in permanent disturbances which at that time, when the civil war had just been terminated, were especially undesirable.

The Russian Orthodox Church took advantage of the relative leniency of the years 1923-28 to consolidate the reforms they had contemplated immediately after the revolution. Since religious education was now forbidden to groups of more than three children, throughout the country, priests, deacons, and earnest laymen collected their forces, distributed the children in groups of three and gave instruction to as many as possible. The young people were exhorted to lead Christian lives. The priests read Russian classics to them and religious works, provided playgrounds and organized excursions; older people were furnished with worthy books which were no longer available in the libraries; mutual aid societies and charitable institutions were established. In 1928, a message of Bishop Eugen of Murom attracted the attention of the Communist papers: the Bishop outlined a program for the Christianization of youth. The plan was spirited and was accommodated to the conditions of the times. A foreign correspondent, usually well informed, implied that the program had been outlined by Acting Patriarch Sergius.[4] In some provinces the movement was known as the "Christomol," or Christian Youth Movement, as opposed to the "Comsomol," or Young Communist Movement. In the province of Tula, about fifty per cent of the youth were said to belong to the Christomol. Time and again the Christomol was victorious over the Comsomol; in the Luga district (province of Petrograd), several members of the Young Communist League resigned, saying that they had become believers; and in the Gdov district of the same province, six of the twelve members of the League joined the church choir.[5]

The fervor of the religious revival of the late twenties shows itself, too, in the efforts of the devout to build new churches in place of those that had been transformed into schools or museums, or destroyed by fire. According to Soviet reports, workers began in 1928 to build a new church in Sobinka (province of Moscow) and another in Viatka (now Kirow). In the district of Odessa, 100,000 rubles were collected for the erection of a new church. Two churches were built in the Novgorod district and four more had been started there when a change in government policy put a halt to the enterprise.[6]

An interesting by-product of overcrowding in big cities emerged through the compulsory redistribution of living space which forced several families to live together in one apartment and to use the same kitchen. Naturally Christian families chose to move to apartments where the other occupants believed as they did; thus little communities were formed where prayers were customary and the Orthodox way of life was followed as far as it could be.

Infuriated by the stamina of churches from which believers could not be wrested, the government launched its second direct attack, that of 1929–30. Many of the aspects of this attack, reported above (chapter II, section 4) may be made intelligible by the facts just discussed, particularly the policy of "cultural strangulation" and the prohibition of religious education.

But again, in this second bombardment, Christians responded with adamant resistance, and again, while open resistance was broken,[7] indomitable moral stubbornness forced the government to a partial retreat in 1930, and a more complete one in 1934.

In the more pacific years that followed (1934–37) attempts were made to do away with the restrictions imposed on the cultural and social life of the churches (see below, section 4) and even to launch a counter-attack. In 1934, many churches which had been closed in 1929–30 were re-opened, not only in remote provinces, but even around Moscow. In Brovky, a station of the South-Eastern Railway, a group of zealous laymen destroyed a platform erected for an anti-religious performance and tried to break it up. In

Kislovodsk (North Caucasus) two days before Easter, anti-religious agitators who had planned an anti-Easter demonstration, were attacked. Toward the end of the year, there were frequent complaints that current issues of the "Godless" remained undistributed through the sabotage of postmen. Early in 1935, in several cities and towns, electric lights were cut off during anti-religious rallies. In 1936, after a representative of the Party, in an unnamed village, had demanded the removal of church bells, a note was pinned to his house threatening that if he pursued his iconoclastic course, his legs would be broken.[8]

The third attack on religion, in 1937–38, was again the result of the uneasy conviction among the ruling clique that religion was still a formidable force, the only force which could oppose the administration at elections. During this assault, the most brutal of all, the beleaguered church "went to the catacombs"; that is to say, it disappeared from the surface, yet continued in its practices and prayers (see below, section 3). This kind of repulse impressed the government as much as the previous ones had; and the attack was ended sixteen months after it had been begun.

2

Active resistance has only been sporadic. Passive resistance, a refusal to relinquish beliefs and a continued participation in church life, has been steady and has proved to be indomitable.

How great is the number of those who oppose official atheism? Exact figures are lacking, but there is sufficient evidence to make an estimate. The census of January 6,

1937, included a question on religious conviction and the government anticipated evidence of its anti-religious achievements.[9] The results of the census were never published, for, it was officially declared, they had been falsified by counter-revolutionists and Trotskyites. The question on religion was omitted from the new census of January 17, 1939.[10] Consequently, it may be suspected that the data gathered in 1937 had been a disappointment. Rumors were persistent that about forty per cent of the population of the U.S.S.R. declared itself to be religious.[11] And who knows how many were not courageous enough to profess their faith when questioned by the census-takers, agents of a government which had proclaimed in advance that the figures would clearly show the disintegration of religion?

In the same year, 1937, Yaroslavsky, the head of the Militant Atheists League, published the following estimate: in the towns more than half the workers, about two thirds of the adult population over sixteen, called themselves atheists. In the villages, however, probably more than half, perhaps two thirds, believed in God.[12] Two years later the monthly journal of the League estimated that half the population in the villages and three quarters in the towns had repudiated religion; but next year, the journal returned to Yaroslavsky's figures for 1937.[13] Since rural population still forms 67% of the total population of the Soviet Union,[14] it may be concluded that 42–47% still are believers.[15]

The number of religious communities was also symptomatic of resistance. In 1937, they numbered 30,000; after the persecution of 1937–38 the number dropped to 20,000, but at the same time it was admitted that the number of unregistered communities had substantially grown. Since

Soviet law requires that at least twenty persons apply for the lease of the church, it may be assumed that there were about half a million "religious activists," that is, people who solemnly declared to local authorities that they were believers.[16]

The distribution of these communities is uneven. There are towns where no churches at all have been left open, or where there have never been churches: these are the new industrial centers built up under the Five-Year Plan. In many towns there are one or two churches left; it has recently been said that there are twenty-five churches in Moscow.[17] Further, there are large rural districts altogether without churches, but there are other provinces where churches are still numerous: in the Moscow province the average is eighteen churches per district, an area inhabited by 50,000 to 100,000 people.[18] However, the geographic distribution of believers does not depend upon churches: practices reported below (section 3) show that there is religious life even where all churches have been closed.[19]

It may reasonably be assumed that the survival of religious feeling is stronger in rural than in urban areas, and among older people than among the younger who have been educated in anti-religious schools, though there is evidence that it is not limited to these groups. In 1937, the Moscow correspondent of the New York *Times* writing of the Easter service in Moscow said:

"A tour of the churches during the night showed a surprising number of young people. . . . At midnight, at the climax of the service, when the priests announced that Christ had risen . . . there were emotional tears in many a youthful eye." [20]

In 1938, the official paper of the Militant Atheists League acknowledged that churches in rural districts were well attended and that young people often observed religious holidays. According to the same journal, a large number of children were seen in the churches of Moscow at the Easter service in 1939; and at Christmas, in the Tambov and Voronezh provinces, many children took part during school hours in processions in honor of the Nativity. In the Tambov province, seven tenths of the children were absent from school on Christmas day and celebrated the Feast in their homes. In Moscow and Tiflis, children with candles in their hands prayed in the churches. In Kursk many children were absent from school during Lent, and attended church and received Holy Communion. In the province of Riazan, many received Holy Communion at the Easter mass, and in the Smolensk province, they took an active part in ceremonies linked with Easter.[21]

Children who do not regularly attend divine services go to church before examinations, at the end of the school year, and so on. Many wear crosses. In one town, school children use inkpots on which are engraved holy images and texts from the Scriptures. In Pessochnoye, a labor suburb of Nizhni Novgorod (now Gorki), school children, meeting a priest, ask for his blessing. In Batum, pupils asked their teacher about the deluge; the teacher explained it as a legend, but the children rejoined by quoting the Bible.[22] In another town, a girl, a senior in high school in good standing and with a thorough knowledge of Marxism, unexpectedly became interested in religion, and a member of the Young Communist League was assigned to show her her folly. He tried to persuade her that a thunderstorm was a natural phenomenon and was not the manoeuvering of celestial powers. The girl replied, "I know that a thunderstorm is an electrical phenomenon but all natural phenomena take place according to laws imposed by God." "There are a great many believers among college and University students. Purely materialistic explanations of metaphysical questions, such as the creation of the world, the beginning of life on the earth, the origin of man, they find inadequate and unsatisfactory and they turn to conclusions adopted by religious minds." [23]

In the provinces of Tsaritsyn (now Stalingrad) and Kuban, young men, returning from military service, were found to have turned to prayer and religious observances. A religious movement among young people, initiated by former monks and nuns, has been set into action in the region around Slaviansk (Donets basin). Active interest in religion among students of the school of education in Viatka (now Kirow) has been reported. In the Mari republic (Middle Volga), during Lent, pioneers did not wear their red neckties; when asked for the reason, they replied that to wear them during the Lenten season would be a sin. In the Tartar republic, an eight-year-old boy declared in school that he believed in God, that he knew prayers, and that he wanted to go to Paradise and not to hell.[24]

Perhaps the very summit was reached by the little school girl who, when asked in the anti-religious school whom she most wanted to be like, replied, "I would like to be as St. Barbara; she has suffered so much for Christ." Who knows whether her desire has not since been realized? [25]

This is rather scattered evidence. But a special investigation, made in the provinces of Moscow and Saratov, showed that more than half the children went to church and prayed at home; many said they liked church services and prayer, although they knew these things were incompatible with their education in the Soviet schools. For the most part, their religious convictions had been handed down to them by their mothers and grandmothers, but sometimes they came from other sources, as, for example, from the wandering minstrels who alternated religious with secular songs.[26] A later report of the accomplishments of anti-religious education contains the statement that in rural districts, at least, children, in spite of their training in atheist schools, attend church, take part in religious ceremonies, and wear crosses. Both parents and children seem to live by the rule, "Study in the anti-religious school of the Soviet State, but do not forget God." [27]

So much for the younger generation in all classes of society. Further data indicate that the working class and even Soviet officials are extremely tenacious of "religious prejudice." Many workers keep icons in their rooms; in the Kaluga district, a worker, asked why he had an icon, answered, "But what if God does exist?" Though they are fined for missing work, many attend religious funerals. Church weddings, baptisms and funerals are frequent in one of the workmen's sections of Ekaterinburg (now Sverdlovsk). At a local meeting of workers held in the vicinity of that city, a Party propagandist asserted confidently that none of the workers attended church. He was interrupted by an old man who said, "You do not know us. I go to church and many others do the same." The dean of the priests in Izhevsk (the capital of the Votiak republic, on the Kama River) is a former worker. At the Kirov factory in

Petrograd (Leningrad), workers read the Bible aloud during the dining recess. In a communal house in the Donets basin, most of the thirty-eight working girls say grace before sitting down to meals. Priests in the Kiev district "try to influence" the Stakhanovists;[28] when the Soviet press says "try," it means they actually do have influence. During the elections to the Supreme Council in the fall of 1937, the secretary of the Party organization in Petrograd reported that workers preferred to go to vespers rather than to the specially arranged electoral meetings. In some cases workers contribute money for the repair of churches.[29]

Instances like these should not be thought exceptional. The journal of the Trade Unions acknowledges a "religious public opinion" in the working class. The following case illustrates the power of this public opinion : when a worker was asked why he had buried a member of his family with church rites, he replied, "It makes no difference to me, but what would have been said in town, if I had not asked a priest to perform the rites?" The same journal explains the neutrality of trade unions on the religious question as the desire to avoid tension between believers and non-believers, an explanation which is intelligible only if one admits that believers are numerous among the workers.[30]

Similar illustrations may be given of the religious tenacity of intellectuals. At Christmas, in 1939, celebrated in Russia on January 7, several civil aviation officers were dismissed for refusing to work. Among them were the chief of the Far Eastern Section, the director of the Moscow school of aviation, and the director of an aviation plant.[31] Not all teachers are atheists even though they are members of the Party or of the Young Communist League; some of them observe religious holidays and participate in church ceremonies. Many permit their pupils to wear crosses, and ask them to remove them if an inspector from the town is expected. In Sukhini-chi (province of Moscow) one teacher was at the head of a group of pupils attending the Easter mass; investigation showed that in place of Marxist theory, he gave his classes religious instruction.[32]

Occasionally officers may be seen at funerals. In a village near Moscow, the priest and the president of the collective farm walked side by side behind the coffin of a deceased member of the farm. In one village of the Middle Volga district, the president of a collective farm solicited signatures for a petition to reopen a church. Another offered peasants old icons instead of wages.[33]

Members of the Communist Party and of the Young Communist League are expected to be active in the struggle, but Yaroslavsky has complained that most members are neutral.[34] In 1937, Kossarev, who was at that time leader of the Young Communist League, said that the new Constitution had been misinterpreted by many members: they claimed, he said, that if the Soviet granted freedom of worship, then it was quite within the law to abstain from anti-religious work.[35]

Sometimes there has been more than neutrality. In the province of Petrograd, the chairman of the local Committee of the Young Communist League was reported to have icons in his home. Frequently, members of the League, after registering their marriage in the Soviet office, proceed to a church wedding. In Armenia, pioneers and members of the League are churchgoers. In the Khoper district, a number of boys and girls, members of the League, abruptly declared that they were believers, and in Novorossisk, a leading member of the League said he could no longer belong to the organization because he had "religious conviction." [36]

Not only members of the League, but even Party members keep icons in their homes. In Pessochnoye, a suburb of Nizhni Novgorod, twelve of the fourteen Party members had icons.[37] The following story was told by *Pravda*: a priest was asked to perform a religious rite in the house of a Communist. He refused, knowing such things were against the regulations. But when he received a written order, he complied. In another village the Party began a prosecution against a Communist who had had his child baptized; the prosecution, however, had to be stopped when it was discovered that almost every member of the Committee had performed some religious rite.[38]

Since in the last few years new contacts have been established between Russians who have submitted to two decades of anti-religious pressure and people who have enjoyed religious freedom, effects of this pressure on different groups have come to light. The following facts are illuminating:

A new church has been opened at Sakhalyan, Manchuria, opposite the important Soviet city of Blagovieschensk, across the river Amur; this was largely the result of the accumulation, in Manchuria, of Russians who had fled persecution in their mother country. At Epiphany, 1940, when bells began to ring in the new church at the Blessings of the Waters, the inhabitants of Blagovieschensk stopped working and began to draw water from the ice-holes believing that, through the Blessing, the water of the Amur River had become temporarily as sacred as the waters of the Jordan.

A detachment of the Red Army ceased to drill and began again when the ceremony was over.[39]

About the same time, when war was being waged in Finland, a number of letters were found on the bodies of Red soldiers killed in action or taken from prisoners; some of these were from relatives of the soldiers, others had been written by themselves but had not been mailed. A study of such letters has shown that time and again the soldiers and their families corresponded in the traditional Russian manner, invoking God and the saints.[40]

In territories annexed by the Soviet State, it was observed that some Red Army soldiers were pious, visited Orthodox and Catholic churches, bought icons, etc. In Bessarabia, Soviet officials appointed by Moscow applied to local priests to have their children baptized and even contributed money for church expenses.[41]

The religious ardor of the urban population, officials of the atheist government, and the Red Army which, incidentally, is entrusted with the task of "enlightening" the young soldiers, is, of course, more than equalled by the average rural community.

In the Yaroslav district, the president of a collective farm was the chairman of the church committee, and as such, he read the Bible to the assembled members of the farm. In many collective farms, people still celebrate Church holidays. Yaroslavsky's aide, Oleschuk, says that during the Christmas season of 1938, members of collective farms did not work for three days.[42] In the village of Vyssokoye, near Nizhni Novgorod, strong religious sentiments were discovered by Party members who visited it in order to prepare for the erection of a monument to the famous aviator Chkalov, a native of the village. On November 24, St. Catherine's day, Divine Service was celebrated in the church and attracted a large crowd. The Communists were told that women named for this Saint desired to celebrate her day. The same occurred on St. Nicholas' day, December 6, when men who were named for the saint paid their homage to him.[43] In the Moscow province, peasants refused to work for three days in order to celebrate the feast of Our Lady of Tikhvin to whom their church was dedicated. On a model collective farm, praised for its anti-religious achievements, one sixth of the members went to confession and took Communion on Easter.[44] From the atheists' point of view, the situation is still more discouraging on the farms which do not belong to the "model" type. For instance, in one of the farms of the Tver (Kalinin) province, all weddings or funerals are presided over by the priest, all children are baptized, members of the farm go to church regularly and exhort their children to do the same.[45] It happened in the Crimea that an official meeting of the members of a collective farm coincided with a prayer meeting; the pastor (it was a Protestant community) expressed in advance his regret that the official meeting would not be held, so certain was he that his flock would obey him rather than the Soviet officials. The Soviet press does not disclose what actually took place; but its silence is significant enough: had the pastor been mistaken, the paper would have triumphantly proclaimed that "religious superstition" had withered away. At any rate, according to a later report, out of one hundred and eight workers on a Crimean farm, only seven worked on the feast of Whitsuntide.[46]

Early in 1939, the official paper of the Commissariat of

Agriculture admitted that religion was still strongly en-
trenched among peasants, and was strengthened by recur-
rent droughts and poor harvests and stimulated by the
skillful adjustment of religious organizations to the new
order. Later on, it was recognized that, during 1939, almost
all church holidays were again celebrated in villages.[47]

The importance of such facts is reinforced by statements
of their increasing frequency. In the summer of 1939, in the
official journal of the Militant Atheists League, we read:
"Icons are *reappearing* in the homes of the members of
collective farms, and of members of the Young Communist
League . . . Similar habits are *reappearing* among Soviet
teachers . . . Members of the Party and of the Young Communist League as well as Stakhanovists display absolute
indifference to the *restoration* of religious practices in their
families, such as the baptism of children, church weddings,
celebration of church holidays, special divine services."
About the same time, the official paper of the Communist
Party wrote: "Many still adhere to the rites and superstitions of the old church, retain belief in religious doctrines
. . . The existence of such a religious ideology offers a fruitful field for the activity of enemies of the people, especially
among the peasantry." One year later, the Militant Atheists
League saw with dismay that the Church's influence was
more vigorous than ever among the masses, particularly
among the youth, that baptism was no longer administered
in secret, that marriages were publicly blessed by priests,
and that funerals had a decidedly religious character.[48]

Again, the official explanation of the phenomenon was
based on the Marxist assumption that religion would necessarily take part in the political struggle, on the side of the

defeated bourgeoisie. Actually these facts indicated that people had begun to understand their strength and the powerlessness of the government to impose upon them any spiritual pattern they did not want to accept. Fear had withered away and, in returning to icons and to religious rites, people published their desire for religious freedom.

### 3

There can be little doubt that millions of Russians believe in God and participate, to a certain extent, in religious rites. Among these are workers, manual and intellectual, young people, and even members of the ruling officialdom; and this is true both in urban and rural districts. It is interesting to investigate how certain forms of religious life were adjusted to the new order.

Foreign correspondents have repeatedly expressed their surprise at the sight of crowds in churches at Christmas and Easter.

"Last night," a report of 1937 read, "far into the early morning hours every remaining [religious] edifice was crowded to capacity with standing devotees, while many times as many worshippers, unable to enter, massed outside, hoping to hear a few words of the ceremony or glimpse the priestly procession announcing the resurrection of the crucified Christ." [49]

"Again as a year ago enormous crowds . . . packed every edifice to suffocation and overflowed into the church yards where would-be worshippers stood in a steady chilly rain or hung to windows to glimpse the midnight ritual." [50]

It is even more striking that similar statements can be cited from Soviet newspapers. In many places, members of collective farms insisted upon celebrating Christmas in the old style. Others, less explicit, merely voted to make January 7 and 8 official days of rest; and city officials chose those days to get leaves of absence in order to go to the country and participate in the rites. The clergy took advantage of such occasions to mix with the younger people in the traditional entertainments of the Russian Christmas season.[51] Immediately after the Finnish war, an instructor in the Militant Atheists League visited certain churches in the Karelian province. On Good Friday, the congregation was a large one and consisted of young and old. At Easter, one church was visited by a hundred and fifty people, another by three hundred; many were not admitted because of lack of space.[52]

Quite recently Yaroslavsky called attention to the perfect "way in which church buildings at present in use are being looked after" giving an idea of "the joy of the believers in making sacrifices and of the practical influence of the Church." He mentioned that "a village parish of about 500 inhabitants in the Volga area collected ten thousand rubles for the renovation of its church." [53]

However, so many churches have been closed that for many people regular church attendance has become impossible. Nevertheless, the creative spirit of the believers has invented remedies.

In Kazan, the church of SS. Peter and Paul has assumed the character of a "central institution" to which children from near and far are brought to be baptized; people wishing to receive Holy Communion are so numerous that they must be divided into groups. On major holidays the church in Ivansyrino (province of Samara) is attended not only by residents of that village but also by people from many neighboring villages. In the native village of Chkalov, the Communists were told that many came to the church from villages where their own churches had been closed. In a district of the Ivanovo province, almost all churches have been closed, but believers ride considerable distances to churches which continue to function.[54]

Sometimes there are mass rites. There are numerous accounts of mass baptisms and mass weddings; during the attack of the years 1937–38 the government took special measures to combat such practices.[55]

Sometimes, too, rites are performed by proxy. In certain villages of the Kiev province, people are obliged to bury their dead without religious services because there are no priests available; but pious relatives take a handful of earth from the grave and send it to a church in Kiev with the request that the burial rites be performed over it; then it is sent back to the relatives to be replaced on the grave which is at last consecrated. Other reports show that such practices are not limited to burials. Children are baptized with water which has been blessed by a priest at some distant place. Young couples are married at the Soviet registry but their wedding rings are sent to the nearest church where the marriage ceremony is read by priests, the rings representing the bride and groom. In the province of Orel, members of a collective farm wanted to hold divine service and pray for a good harvest; as there was no longer a priest for the village, one of the women was sent to the city of Orel for holy water. The peasants went to the fields with icons and blessed the soil with the water.[56]

Of course these practices were not satisfactory, and the

appearance of "travelling priests" was probably the most consoling aid to the revival of religious sentiment. Travelling priests were first mentioned in 1934; they appeared at Easter time and were gladly received by the population; in many places divine service was held in churches which had been closed because they had no priests. Gradually, these priests became numerous. From the Smolensk province comes this story: "A travelling salesman appeared in a village. Soon it became known that he was also a priest. The inhabitants were very pleased, for there was none in their village. Many took advantage of the opportunity to have their children baptized; among them were children of school age and even two pioneers." [57] The official journal of the Militant Atheists reports: "A number of priests travel from place to place carrying everything necessary for the performance of religious rites; often they also help the inhabitants by giving them advice, nursing the sick, and so on." [58] Toward the end of 1937, a campaign against travelling priests was carried out by order of Yezhoff, Commissar of the Interior. Bishop Sergius and a priest, Dementi, who was looked upon as a saint, were arrested.[59] Since the fall of Yezhoff (December, 1938) there have been no such raids, but it appears from statements in the official press that the government still considers itinerant clergy highly undesirable.

Another phenomenon which has recently appeared in Soviet Russia is the "revival of catacombs," the springing up of secret (that is, unregistered) groups. One such group, numbering about a hundred and fifty, among them members of the Young Communist League, was reported in Kolomna; they were called "ravine worshippers." A

"League for the Revival of the Church" has been discovered in Viatka, with ramifications throughout the district. In Murom, a priest created "catacombs" under his house where people gathered to pray and to bemoan the plight of religion. A group of "escapers" is known to have secret places of refuge in the Udmurt district.[60]

Secret monasteries have also been established. The Metropolitan of Nizhni Novgorod (Gorki) gave his blessing to the enterprise and a number of such monasteries were soon operating. Examples are numerous. In Tver (Kalinin), a pious woman bought an old house, repaired it and presented it to a community of the "Reverers of Father John of Cronstadt." Monks of a destroyed cloister in Slaviansk organized a "holy home" where priests and monks found refuge and were joined by many young people. The same thing took place after the destruction of the Tikhvin monastery near Penza. A secret monastery has been discovered in the Smolensk province, where the monks concealed their rule by working in Soviet institutions.[61] Somewhere in Ukraine, a Catholic monastery called "Sertsano" was run by Father Nascressensky; it was ostensibly a dining room. Father Budnitsky has organized two Catholic monasteries in Kiev and Zhitomir.[62]

Not only a secret monastery, but even a secret Theological Academy survived in Moscow until 1938. It was headed by Archbishop Batholomey and had a non-registered church which was called the St. Peter Monastery. Several boys joined the group. The prior was severe and enforced the rigorous statutes of the famous "Optina Pustyn." His orders were faithfully obeyed; frequently he directed boys to study in Soviet institutions of higher learning. Advanced religious instruction was given in the monastery itself, and graduates were ordained as priests.[63]

The clergy is resigned to secrecy. Its members obtain employment as workers or officials, and continue to hold religious services and to preach in secret. "Nothing marks them off from the population, they work like the humblest workers," complains the monthly journal of the Militant Atheists League. Sometimes dramatic stiuations evolve: for instance, when the head of the largest State hospital in Tashkent died, he was buried, to the great astonishment of the Communists, in the robes of an Orthodox archbishop, for such he was, in Central Asia. In Nizhni Novgorod, a high official was at the same time the prior of a secret monastery. In a remote province, a meteorologist was a student in a secret theological academy to which he contributed ten percent of his earnings.[64]

Secrecy was imposed also on many laymen, especially during the early thirties when discrimination against believers was particularly ruthless. Because of mutual suspicion and the impossibility of being sure that even one's consort was not an agent of the secret police, extraordinary situations were created. A case is reported in which both husband and wife were believers but concealed the fact from one another. When a child was born to them, first the mother had it baptized, and, a few days later, the father went to the priest to have the same child baptized. He was astonished when the priest refused to perform the rite and told him why. The couple had the joy of learning that both were believers.[65]

Other cases illustrate the resumption of practices peculiar to the Russian religious tradition. In 1937, Kossarev told of

" 'rejuvenations' of icons and of resumed pilgrimages to holy springs." Rumors concerning miracles and religious apparitions circulate in all parts of the country. As in old times, on big holidays, beggars gather in front of churches and beg for alms in the name of Christ from passers-by, and one may meet monks in their robes even in the streets of Petrograd (Leningrad).[66]

### 4

These facts touch on the very kernel of Church activity. Others disclosed that the Church has succeeded in circumventing some restrictions imposed on it by the legislation of the Soviet government, especially in the cultural and social sphere. How do we know it? We know it from frequent cases reported in the Soviet press, and some are interesting enough to be repeated.

In Kagalnik, near Rostov, a recently repaired church faces an empty Red club. For the last few years, it has been the priest, not the public library, who has supplied the villagers with books.[17] In the Tartar Republic, a priest organized religious discussions and invited atheists; almost all the members of the Young Communist League attended. In Berezki, West Siberia, the church committee organized a club; in the Petrograd district, theatrical societies and choirs. Choirs begin their recitals with secular music, but gradually shift to religious songs. Attendance is large. In the Tver (Kalinin) province, priests got together groups of young people and told them of things which interested them and which were unknown to Soviet teachers. Near Borovichi (Tver province), the priest persuaded the youth to start a football team and he played on it himself. Sometimes priests read to their congregations from Russian classics, inserting prayers and hymns between the chapters. In some places, priests organize excursions for young people and do this much more efficiently than the leaders of the Young Communist League. Priests have established banks for mutual assistance; transactions in these are based on confidence in the priest, so that authorities cannot even prove their existence. Sometimes priests, rather than Soviet lawyers, are asked for legal advice.[68]

Compare these facts with the clauses of the decree of April 8, 1929, and you will see that they are in direct opposition to the law. But no law can be enforced if important sections of the population are antagonistic to it, and this was the fate of the law which introduced "cultural strangulation"; if the law had been enforced, thousands of people would have been arrested and tried; but gradually local authorities wearied and stopped harassing the offenders.

Church activity is impossible without material means. The sweeping decree of 1918, confirmed in 1929, prohibited regular collections of money or any assistance to Church organizations from State institutions. Today, in many places, this prohibition has been waived. Collecting money for the benefit of churches is common. According to Yaroslavsky, collective farms, the strongholds of socialism in the countryside, are beginning to support churches. Work brigades prepare fuel for the churches and are given credit for the time they spend. General meetings of members of the farms claim the right to vote certain sums of money for the maintenance of churches, and the administrative boards of the farms carry out such [illegal] decisions.[69]

In some villages, priests have applied for membership in the collective farms. They have been accepted and are remunerated for their religious work as regular members; in other words, they are given a share in the net profit; their income, *i.e.,* the fees of the parishioners for the performance of certain rites, has been "socialized," and this means that those who request a special divine service pay a sum to the treasurer of the farm. In some cases, land has been allotted to the priest—probably little plots around his house, for this is all that a member of a collective farm may possess individually. Occasionally horses or trucks are given to the priests so that they may visit remote parts of their parishes. Church buildings are repaired by the farm laborers, and are provided with fuel and electric light. To facilitate church-going (which means, of course, increase in church income), in some collective farms horses are placed at the disposal of believers if they have to go to a distant church. According to a recent report, collective farm managers lend their best horses to parents who must go to remote churches to have their babies baptized.[70]

## 5

Believers have resisted persecution; they have preserved faith and have done their best to help the tormented Churches and the clergy. How far have they been able to preserve the traditional structure of the Churches? On this question material is scarce, and only tentative conclusions may be drawn.

Only a few denominations have preserved their central organizations. Among them are the two branches of the

Orthodox Church (the Patriarchal and the Living Church). Roman Catholics have kept their allegiance to the Holy See, but, in practice, their local organizations have been compelled to go almost altogether into the catacombs. The years of uninterrupted persecution have served to eradicate rivalry among the denominations. Dogmatic controversies have almost stopped; a kind of coalition of believers is sometimes spoken of by their enemies. It has been reported that the conflict between the Patriarchal and the Living Church is no longer very bitter; that there are no longer quarrels between the Orthodox Church and the Old Ritualists; and, especially, that there is understanding between the Greek Orthodox and the Roman Catholics.[71]

Significant changes have taken place within the Greek Orthodox Church. Its structure has become more democratic than formerly. There is a certain "presbyterian" tendency, partly because of the difficulty of communicating with the diocesan sees, partly because some priests have seized the opportunity which presented itself during the 1937–38 attack against the bishops, and have assumed a position of semi-independence incompatible with Church tradition.[72] On the other hand, in districts where all churches have been closed and all priests imprisoned or exiled, the flocks manage without them; pious men and women read aloud the Holy Writ and the Liturgical books (with the exception of the Eucharist).[73] This has always been the custom of the more radical groups of the Old Ritualists.

Sometimes the departure from tradition goes still further.

New groups with peculiar notions have formed: the "non-performers of rites" are religious people who observe popular customs connected with church holidays, but who sometimes join the Militant Atheists League, attend anti-religious lectures, and explain that they enjoy the meetings because at the meetings religious problems are discussed. Another group call themselves the "concealers," for though they continue to perform religious rites, they do so covertly. There are finally "silent people" who never answer official questionnaires on religion; they do not take part in elections and, in 1937, they tried to avoid the census because a question on religious belief was asked; they do not allow their children to go to school, since education is anti-religious.[74]

A qualified observer admits the religious revival in Russia, especially in the course of the last three years, but emphasizes that, "to a large extent, the movement has developed outside the framework of the existing Churches, under the guise of study circles and discussion groups, often conducted, for the sake of convenience, within the framework of some approved Soviet organization. The younger generation reared under the new system is chiefly involved, especially university youth and a section of the intelligentsia. It may best be described as a trend, rather than a unified movement, of people going to rediscover in Christianity the answer to those fundamental questions which the official teaching has failed to provide. They are not anti-Soviet. For the most part, they accept the new social order unquestioningly. But their intellects hunger for something more than the meager fare of dialectical materialism. The purge [of the years 1936–38] has clearly disclosed the necessity for basing love, loyalty, justice, honesty, and all the basic ethical concepts of human society on something more than class interest." [75]

In summing up this meager evidence, it may be said that very likely the Greek Orthodox Church has temporarily lost more than religion: [76] whereas about half the population is still religious, a substantial number, deliberately or through necessity, have abandoned the formerly Established Church and formed new groups, usually of a quite local character and small size.

Neither the official structure nor the dogma of the Greek Orthodox Church has been altered, and it is noteworthy that the Living Church had to abandon almost altogether its plans of reforming Orthodoxy. However, a certain tendency to simplify the rites has been definitely shown; this was necessitated by the transfer of divine service from church buildings to private dwellings or catacombs. That there has been no demand for this simplification on the part of the people may be seen from the fact that when conditions are favorable, divine service is as splendid as possible; the people continue to like well-trained and large choirs, and efficient priests do their best to provide talented singers and, if possible, to recruit good conductors. In the late thirties, individual priests have accomplished what baffled Patriarch Tikhon in the early twenties: a number of Church holidays have been moved to the "rest days" of the official week, and everyone has a chance to attend services.[77]

Compromises have naturally been made during these more than twenty years in the bosom of an atheist State. A large part of the Church members wished to come to terms with the government, in so far as this was possible without abrogating dogmas or institutions. As early as 1934, Yaroslavsky wrote: "Members of the Church speak of building up socialism with God's help. Priests welcome the slogan of prosperity to all the members of collective farms; but they add that this should not make people forget God. In one village the priest asked for permission to take part in the distribution of the Soviet loan; when the campaign was finished, it appeared that he had collected three times as much money as the officer of the Red Corner." [78] A few days later, the official journal of the League wrote: "We have investigated villages near Novgorod and Pskov and have come across the following facts: icons have been removed from the walls, but are hidden in chests . . . Sometimes one of the corners of a peasant's room is decorated with icons, and another with pictures of Party leaders," [79] indicative of a desire to combine religious faith with loyalty to the new regime.

In 1937, Kossarev said that the plan of religionists was to reconcile religion with the State, letting God penetrate into the framework of socialism. [80] During the elections to the Supreme Soviet, a priest offered the local Soviet his services in interpreting the electoral law. [81] The revival of religion has been explained partially by the acceptance of "red color" by the clergy; they sometimes engage in propaganda for the progress of socialist reconstruction and praise the Soviet government. [82] They can go so far as to give special privileges to the "enthusiasts" of the Soviet regime. Thus, in Tsaritsyn (Stalingrad) it was announced that the members of the Stakhanov movement would have their Easter meats and cakes blessed before those of other people.[88] Such practices make them invulnerable to attack by the Commissariat of the Interior, the Party, and the Young Communist League which find no weapons to combat them.

However, it is not so much compromises which have helped the Churches to survive; more important has been the spirit of sacrifice among the clergy and laymen. One example will be sufficient: during the periods of bitter attack, in 1922–23 and 1929–30, the government hoped to destroy the Orthodox Church by wholesale arrests of bishops. However, the plan was impracticable, for an arrested bishop was immediately replaced. Later on it was learned that, during these years, in every diocese, there were numerous consecrated bishops, instructed to continue their current mode of existence but to be ready to occupy the bishop's chair after the arrest of the men who preceded them on the list. There were nowhere lacking men who agreed to be consecrated despite the certainty of arrest and exile or even death as a consequence.

Sacrifices have been made by laymen as well, by those unknown men and women who served as members of the official "twenties" of the religious groups, who contributed to the needs of the churches and of the clergy, who continued to come to church when their social status was imperiled, who secretly gave their children religious education and who, in individual cases, actively resisted desecration and blasphemy.

Equally important has been the spirit of love in the faithful members of the Churches. Let us cite a few cases reported by the Soviet press which give insight into methods of religious propaganda under most unfavorable conditions.

In a big village, the atheists believed they had uprooted religion after closing the two churches and expelling the priests. But one of the priests clandestinely returned; he gathered children and told them stories from the Bible, which interested them far more than what they learned at school. This village school, incidentally, was one of the many where no one looked out for the children; the teachers were harsh; no textbooks were available. The priest became popular among the children; they spoke of him enthusiastically to their mothers, and some began to visit him; very soon he became the most respected person in the village.[84]

A member of the Young Communist League, for sport, asked the priest to lend him a robe for a theatrical performance. The priest complied. The astonished young man came to church; asked for an explanation, he said that he had come a few minutes before the end of the divine service and that he had come on business. Later he paid a visit to the priest and asked him to allow a group of pilgrims to spend the night in the church, since no other accommodations were available. The priest refused, saying that Church regulations did not permit church buildings to be used as living quarters, but commended the young man on his solicitude for the pilgrims; the young man became one of the secret believers.[85]

In another region, the influence of religion became so widespread among Young Communists that the local Committee of the League instituted an investigation to discover the reason. From friendly chats with individual members, the Committee gathered that they were attracted by the kindness of religious people who were always willing to listen to the young, quite unlike the Young Communist leaders who were sardonic and dictatorial.[86]

## FOOTNOTES TO CHAPTER THREE

(1) The events of the years 1917–21 have been described on the basis of direct observation by the author who spent these years in Petrograd. He first described his experience in "Destiny of the Russian Culture" (in Russian), *Russkaya Mysl,* Prague, 1922.

(2) Sir Bernard Pares, *Russia,* Penguin Books, New York, 1940, p. 172.

(3) This statement may amaze those who consider, on the basis of declarations of Communist leaders, that their rule over Russia is "enlightened despotism," supporting the intellectual forces. However, a government ought to be judged not on the basis of what it says, but of what it does; and the Communist government actually has destroyed the intellectual forces which it has found in Russia, despite the dominance, among them, of a "progressive tendency."

(4) The program of Bishop Eugen, reported to *Vozrozhdeniye* (published in Russian, in Paris), July 28, 1928, consisted of the following points: 1) special preparation of children for first confession, especially the teaching of the *credo;* 2) special sermons addressed to children; 3) talks with parents concerning the Christian education of children; 4) organization of lectures and excursions for children and youth; 5) organization of athletic teams; 6) material help to needy children, and 7) organization of teams of adult believers, to take care of children during the harvest season, and to use the opportunity to give them some information about the chief events of the Old and New Testament. It was additionally recommended to create "Child Jesus" and "Virgin Mary" groups; one of the weekdays was to be designated the "children's day," and one of the big holidays should be chosen as "the children's holiday."

(5) B. 1928, No. 32; P., May 9, 1928.

(6) B. 1928, No. 23; P., May 9, 1928, and June 7, 1928.

(7) In the village Velezhanka (location unknown), the local Soviet decided to close the church and to transform it into a school. But when a commission arrived to carry out the decision, believers began to sound the tocsin. A crowd of 2,000 gathered and prevented the commission from closing the church. The crowd dispersed only after the chief of the local police had promised that the church would not be closed (I., May 16, 1929).

(8) B. 1934, No. 14; K.P., November 15, 1936.

(9) The population was sometimes worried by the question of reli-

gion. An old woman asked the census-taker whether all believers would be expelled from Moscow; many people asked why they should give any information about their religious attitude; some people tried to evade the question saying that they believed in the Soviet regime. P., January 5, 1937; K.P., January 4, 1937.

(10) *Cf.* N. S. Timasheff, "The Population of Soviet Russia," *Rural Sociology*, September, 1940.

(11) *Journal des Débats*, June 9, 1937.

(12) *On Antireligious Propaganda* (in Russian), Moscow, 1937. It is highly probable that Yaroslavsky's estimate was based on the findings of the suppressed census of 1937. In the course of 1937–38, Soviet leaders made many quantitative statements which were more or less obviously connected with that census.

(13) A. 1939, No. 5, 1940, Nos. 2 and 13.

(14) *Cf.* N. S. Timasheff, article quoted *supra*, note 10.

(15) Making one of the earliest estimates of the number of atheists, Yaroslavsky acknowledged that, perhaps, a significant fraction of the atheists were not good atheists at all (B. 1934, No. 10).

(16) V.P. 1937, No. 6; K.P., August 8, 1937; B. 1937, No. 10; A. 1939, No. 6 and 1940, No. 2. According to *Soviet War News* (published in London), of August 22, 1941, in 1941 religious communities again numbered 30,000. If there actually has been an increase, it may be explained (1) by the addition of the parishes located in newly annexed territories, and (2) by the renewed registration of some religious communities which, in 1927–38, went to the "catacombs."

(17) *Journal des Débats*, June 4, 1937.

(18) A. 1938, No. 7. Local authorities are not always quite sure about their "achievements" concerning the closing of churches. Very illuminating is the following case: "The town Soviet of Nizhni Tagil (Ural province) pretends that only two churches are open in its district; actually, 20 churches continue functioning" (K.P., November 15, 1936).

(19) A. 1939, No. 6.

(20) *New York Times*, May 3, 1937.

(21) B. 1938, Nos. 16, 26, 28; 1939, No. 14; U.G., October 23, 1938; The Bolshevist Peasant Manual, March, 1941.

(22) V.P. 1937, No. 6; K.P., May 5 and June 9, 1937; B. 1939, No. 17; A. 1939, No. 4 and 1940, No. 7.

(23) P., March 25, 1940; B., April 5, 1941.

(24) Z.K.P., March 30, 1937; K.P., December 23, 1938; B. 1939, No. 5; A. 1940, No. 7.

(25) Stakhnovich, *Zapiski Bezboznika* (in Russian), Leningrad, 1934.

(26) A. 1935, No. 1.

(27) U.G., April 9, 1939.

(28) See chapter II, note 28.

(29) P., December 14, 1936; A. 1937, No. 6; L.P., July 20, 1937; P.S. 1937, No. 23; V.P. 1937, No. 6; B. 1939, Nos. 15 and 17; B.(m) 1940, No. 10.

(30) V.P., 1937, No. 6.

(31) Wire from Moscow (Agence Havas, January 22, 1932).

(32) Z.K.P., March 18, 1937; U.G., October 26 and 27, 1937; N. S. Timasheff, "The Church and the World in Soviet Russia," *Vozrozhdeniye* (see note 4), June 15, 1935.

(33) V.C., June 26, 1937.

(34) P.S. 1938, No. 7.

(35) P., April 15, 1937. Actually, the new Constitution merely repeated the statements of the Constitution of the RSFSR of May 11, 1925, as amended in 1929. However, the restatement of an old proposition under new circumstances sometimes makes this proposition sound new.

(36) B. 1937, No. 29; 1939, Nos. 14 and 15; K.P., November 15, 1936, and June 5, 1939; P., March 25, 1940.

(37) V.P. 1937, No. 6; B. 1937, No. 30; P.S. 1938, No. 7.

(38) P., June 4, 1935.

(39) *Posslednya Novosti* (published in Russian, in Paris), January 21, 1940. The Soviet papers which published the report were unavailable.

(40) Personal communication of Mr. V. M. Zenzinoff who had the opportunity to read and to classify a great number of such letters.

(41) H. Iswolsky. "The Russian Church and the War" 2, *The Commonweal*, 1941, No. 26.

(42) B. 1937, No. 30; 1938, No. 23; 1939, No. 3; A. 1939, Nos. 4 and 7.

(43) B. 1939, No. 2.

(44) B.(m) 1941, No. 1.

(45) A. 1938, No. 7.

(46) Oleschuk, *A New Phase in the Struggle against Religion*, Leningrad, 1938; B. 1939, No. 17.

(47) S.Z., January 8, 1939; B. 1939, No. 10.

(48) B. 1939, No. 24; P., August 20, 1939; *The Tablet* (London), June 15, 1940; A. 1940, No. 5.

(49) *New York Times*, May 3, 1937.

(50) *Ibid.*, April 24, 1938.

(51) B. 1939, No. 3.

(52) A. 1940, No. 2.

(53) A. 1941, No. 5.

(54) B. 1939, No. 18; V.C., June 26, 1937; A. 1940, No. 2.

(55) B. 1939, No. 11.

(56) B. 1939, Nos. 11, 12, 18 and 25; A. 1938, No. 11; 1939, Nos. 5 and 6; 1940, No. 2.

(57) K.P., March 1, 1938.

(58) B. 1939, No. 12.

(59) *Ibid.*

(60) B. 1938, Nos. 31 and 33.

(61) T., December 20, 1937; P.S. 1938, No. 7; B. 1939, No. 16.

(62) A. 1938, No. 3; 1939, Nos. 6 and 10.

(63) B. 1939, No. 3.

(64) T., December 20, 1937; *Vozrozhdeniye* (see note 4), April 12, 1936; A. 1939, Nos. 3 and 5.

(65) Personal communication of Dr. Leiper, Secretary of the World's Council of Evangelic Churches.

(66) P., April 15, 1937; P.S. 1938, No. 7; B. 1938, No. 25; 1939, No. 16. The rejuvenation of icons is a phenomenon which has been frequently reported during the first five years of Communist rule. It consisted of a gradual restoration of the original colors of icons affected by smoke or inclemencies of the weather and was considered by many people as a miracle.

(67) P., April 11, 1935.

(68) B. 1937, No. 30; 1938, No. 11; K.P., May 18, 1937; U.G., October 26 and 27, 1937; K.G., November 15, 1938.

(69) P.S. 1938, No. 7; 1939, No. 11.

(70) A. 1939, Nos. 6, 7, and 10; B. 1939, No. 16.

(71) A. 1938, Nos. 2 and 5; 1939, No. 6.

(72) A. 1939, No. 6.

(73) A. 1930, No. 2.

(74) B. 1939, Nos. 6 and 9.

(75) *Christian Science Monitor,* August 2, 1941.

(76) According to *Soviet War News,* August 22, 1941, two thirds of the believers continued to belong to the Greek Orthodox Church.

(77) A. 1938, No. 7; 1939, Nos. 5 and 6; B.(m) 1936, No. 6.

(78) P., February 26, 1934.

(79) B. 1934, No. 10.

(80) P., April 15, 1937.

(81) A. 1938, Nos. 5 and 7.

(82) B. 1937, No. 30; 1939, No. 12; K.P., April 1, 1939; A. 1939, No. 6.

(83) K.P., April 23, 1937.

(84) Z.K.P., February 26, 1937.

(85) K.P., March 15, 1937.

(86) K.P., March 11, 1937.

# CHAPTER FOUR

# The Recognition of a Failure

## I

RELIGION HAS NOT BEEN DESTROYED IN RUSSIA. In the struggle between the old Christian faith and the new Communist order, about half the population is still Christian, demands religious liberty and is opposed to religious persecution; most of the other half is neutral.

The Communist government always knew that its antireligious policy lacked public support and frankly admitted this whenever it was compelled to retreat. When, in 1923, the first onslaught was petering out, the Central Committee of the Trade Unions [1] declared: "The final liberation of workers from religious superstition may take place only as the result of durable educational activity directed towards inculcating the principles of materialism in the masses at large; the struggle against religion will not be terminated by casual decrees and administrative coercion, but by persistent and systematic propaganda for Marxism."

One year later, the XIII Congress of the Communist Party stated: "It is necessary to liquidate all attempts to uproot religion by administrative measures, such as the closing of churches. Anti-religious propaganda in the countryside must be limited to the materialistic explanation of those natural and social phenomena which frequently recur in the peasants' life. It is especially important to avoid anything which could jar the religious sentiments of the believers; such sentiments can be extirpated only by patient work in the course of decades."

In the Fall of 1924, at a meeting of the Central Committee of the Party of Georgia, one member exclaimed: "Today there is no intelligent Party member who would not agree that our anti-religious activity has been overdone. All talks that peasants do not want their churches and voluntarily close them are self-delusion. We must make up for our mistake and give the peasants back the keys of their churches, granting them full liberty to pray as they like. However, at this point we shall meet resistance on the part of our local comrades." [2]

These quotations pretty definitely establish that, in 1923–24, the Communist Party was fully aware that its anti-religious policy was thoroughly unpopular. But the lesson was gradually forgotten and the second direct attack, that of 1929–30, took place as if the failures of 1921–23 had never occurred.

Events repeated themselves with astonishing similarity. The gradual mitigation of the anti-religious policy, first in 1930, and then in 1934–35, was accompanied by the same admissions. By issuing the decree of March 15, 1930, the government admitted that the church closures had been contrary to the wishes of the population. By abolishing the teaching of Marxism in schools (April 2, 1934) the Central Committee of the Party admitted that it irritated all the students. By explaining the prohibition of anti-religious carnivals and processions, Yaroslavsky confessed that these processions served only to increase religious sentiment. The joy of the population when they were granted permission to light the Christmas trees was recorded by the Soviet newspapers.

However, once more, recognition of failure did not prevent the Communist government from launching a third attack, the truly Neronian outrages of the years 1937–38. And, once more, in 1939, statements by leaders of the anti-religious movement acknowledged the failure.

"The activity of the League of Militant Atheists has proved fruitless; it has increased dissatisfaction, but not with religion or with the clergy. Among members of collective farms the dissatisfaction with the official atheism is growing. This is the reason why parents frequently refuse to send children to school and why in many cases children refuse to attend school." Curtailing church attendance, it was said in another paper, has not influenced the manners of children. Arrests of religionists, says another source, have not weakened the prevalence of belief.[3] Perhaps the most revealing confession is the following, on the persecution of 1937–38: "During the previous years a number of priests and religionists were declared counter-revolutionaries and many more churches were closed; but it now appears that in many cases this was carried out by the enemies of the people in order to increase the hostility to the Soviet government." [4] About that time, "enemies of the people" were identified with the followers of Bukharin and Trotsky. Certainly, the followers of Bukharin and Trotsky had nothing to do with the arrests; but they were always resurrected when a tremendous blunder was committed by the government and excuses were necessary.

Never before had the enemies of religion so frankly admitted their defeat. Furthermore, in 1939, in contrast with

the earlier withdrawals, leaders of the anti-religious movement had to recognize that the believers were not the
wicked or ignorant men they should have been according
to Marxist theory. It was conceded frequently that Christians were not as black as they were painted; their faith
in God was not opposed to a respect for science or to a desire for cooperation with the agencies for public welfare;
they were not fanatics; religion was able to convert workers,
peasants and even members of the Stakhanov movement,
because the Church was no longer what it had been in the
past.[5]

Summing up, about the end of 1939, one of the official
papers of the government said: "It is much more difficult
to uproot religion from the consciousness of the workers
than to liberate them from the exploitation of capitalists." [6]

### 2

About this time, another bulwark of Communist leadership began to totter. The agency entrusted with the task
of extirpating religion, the famous League of the Militant
Atheists, was discovered to be in a state of pathetic and
thorough disintegration. Its decay was first recognized in
1937, before the beginning of the last persecution; it de-
clined still further during this persecution and on into the
era of the New Religious Policy.

In 1933, the League numbered five and a half million
members; according to the Five Year Anti-religious Plan,
an enrollment of fifteen million was expected by 1937. The
facts were different. In 1937, the leaders of the League
spoke of two million, but the executive secretary of the
organization considered the actual membership to be still

smaller. Provincial committees which had been established in 1931 ceased to exist at all. And where they existed officially, instructors, sent on behalf of the Central Committee, sometimes had difficulty in locating their headquarters.[7]

Symptoms of decay in the League were discernible as early as 1935: a reporter was sent by one of the Moscow journals to Smolensk to study the progress of anti-religious work. He was unable to find the office of the Provincial Committee of the Militant Atheists League and called on the provincial branch of the Young Communist League which, officially, had to support it. His query about the Atheist League was met with ironical smiles: no one was interested in anti-religious activity.[8] In the province of Archangel, the only circular letter mailed in 1935 to the local cells by the provincial headquarters of the League was returned from most places with a notation that the addressee was unknown.[9]

During the last persecution, 1937-38, central authorities sent out instructions to intensify the activity of the League, but these were ineffective. Local organizations were satisfied with attracting new members, collecting dues, issuing special anti-religious badges and copying circular letters from headquarters. During one of the few anti-religious conferences held in recent years, the chairman said that he had been appointed by mistake, that he did not see any progress and that actually the members of the League accomplished nothing.[10] In the Petrograd (Leningrad) province, an attempt was made to revive the local organization of the League, but the provincial conference stated three months later that the attempt was futile. At the conference, the secretary of the provincial organization exclaimed bitterly that all the anti-religious work in the province was in his pocket: that is, that it consisted of a few trifling papers.[11] The same thing happened in Chelyabinsk (in the Ural province). In January an instructor arrived from the center, spent about one month there, göt results—or reported that he had; but in June another report reached the central organization saying that things were as bad as ever. Another instructor was sent and reported that he had reorganized the local cells. But a few month later, when a provincial conference was convoked, it appeared that no one could represent Chelyabinsk, since no anti-religious workers were known to exist there.[12]

The situation did not improve in 1939 or 1940. In May, 1939, Oleschuk, vice-president of the League, acknowledged that in the whole of the USSR there were no more than ten clubs in which anti-religious propaganda was well organized. Later in the year, a survey was published in the monthly journal of the League; it turned out that in such an important industrial center as Izhevsk (on the Kama River) there was no anti-religious work at all; in the province of Nizhni Novgorod (Gorki), cells of the League abounded, but did nothing; in Irbit (Western Siberia), the district committee of the League did not meet for a single session in the course of the year. Early in 1940, one could read that "the enemies of anti-religious work had obtained that, in the majority of provinces, there is no anti-religious work at all. Local cells have ceased to exist, lecturers are unavailable." [13] In September, 1940, the Central Committee of the League convoked a special conference. The report delivered to the conference acknowledged that anti-religious propaganda was dying; the Party and the Young Communist League no longer co-operated. Members of the conference could not say anything that might mitigate the pessimistic findings of the Central Committee.[14]

Under such circumstances, it is almost of no consequence that League membership has numerically increased: 2,292,000 members were reported in 1939; 2,983,000 in 1940; and 3,450,000 in 1941.[15] Three and a half million drones: this seems to be an adequate description.

What are the causes of the gigantic failure? First of all, as the leaders themselves admit, the League has obviously recruited the scum of Communist society. "The local organizations have enrolled scoundrels, individuals with a dark past." In the Azerbaijan republic, the members of the League are picked up at random. No one really understands anti-religious work; all are inclined to fraud; the activity is chaotic; vast plans are elaborated, but no one cares to execute them. . . . In Rostov, the local Party Committee imposes anti-religious activity on "those Party members who proved to be unfit for anything else or those who are to be punished for some offense against discipline; anti-religious activity is considered a kind of dirty work." Many local authorities throughout the country claim that the proceedings of the League are based on swaggering and fraud.[16]

The second reason for failure is the ineptitude of the propagandists. A few illustrations will show how things are.

"A lecture was delivered in the Moscow province. The topic was 'Christmas and the class nature of religion'. Only a few 'activists' had patience enough to stay to the end;

the greater part of the audience left during the first half. Nevertheless, another lecture was announced in the same locality, concerning itself with 'The New Year and the class nature of religion.' The result was even worse: the audience left after 15 minutes. Commonly, such lectures simply bore the public." [17]

"In Bezhitsa (Tver province), a teacher delivered a lecture on Easter and the customs accompanying it. When peasants asked him how such customs originated, he could say nothing better than that they had been invented by priests. Quite naturally, the peasants left the room in a state of intense dissatisfaction." [18]

At a meeting organized for a group of chemists, the lecturer stated: "Persia formerly was Turkey, but in general all Persians are Turks." He was corrected by the audience. He continued his lecture by contrasting Christianity with Roman Catholicism. When asked if these were two different religions, he said that they were. At this point the audience lost patience, and the propagandist was thrown out. Investigations suggest the explanation: local organizations do not pay lecturers; consequently experts are unwilling to lecture; they are replaced by "inspectors of atheism"; but the remuneration of those officials is very small and the positions are taken by half-educated hacks who are sometimes almost illiterate.[19]

Speaking in general of the propagandists, the papers of the League say: "The lecturers talk nonsense; what they say may be called 'anti-religious miracles.' " And further: "The lecturers are not so much selected by the League as enrolled from among those offering their services; such applications come in especially about the time of Summer vacation; the applicants are only interested in the amount of their remuneration." [20]

At the conference held in September, 1940 (mentioned above), the reporter once more saw that the lecturers had no talent and had received an inadequate training.[21]

Often the intellectual revival embarrasses the lecturers with difficult questions. They are, for instance, asked, "Why are our youth so rough? Why have we so many neglected children?" These are wounding questions in a Communist society where there should be no laziness or neglect. Sometimes members of the audience point out that recent discoveries in physics are incompatible with the official materialism, or that men are able to perceive only phenomena, but not the essence of things (Kant's philosophy which is counter to official dogma). Faced with such questions the propagandists are completely at sea.[22]

It is therefore unimportant that in 1939 two hundred thousand and in 1940 two hundred and thirty thousand anti-religious lectures were delivered throughout the country.[23] According to official statements, "in most cases the meetings organized by the League are attended by atheists who no longer need any anti-religious propaganda."[24] Commenting on a recent report by a provincial Committee of the Militant Atheists League, the League's monthly journal admitted that the members did not try to influence Christians, for the very good reason that they feared defeat in discussions of religion. Summing up, it may be said that the ambition of the Communist State was to limit the Church to addressing its own members; actually it is the League of Militant Atheists which can address only its own members, who are the dregs of Communist society.

3

The real cause for the failure of the League does not appear in official reports. It is surely the complete lack of anti-religious enthusiasm in the League itself which has been transformed into a bureaucratic agency unable to struggle with the flaming faith of its opponents. Instead of anti-religious zeal, there is complacency or indifference.

Complacency emerges whenever the government abstains from too resolutely fighting religion. In 1928 *Pravda* reported:

"Up to the present day, there was a kind of peaceful co-existence between the monks of the Oran monastery (province of Nizhni Novgorod) and the local Communists. Every morning two groups of men left the cells, all bells ringing: one was composed of monks in their robes, the other of men with folders and portfolios in their hands: they were the leading workers of the local Soviet. Communists did not oppress the monks: 'Why should we do so,' the secretary of the Party cell used to say; 'They are plain people, only in robes.' The chairman of the Soviet added that the monks were very useful people; never did they refuse to help needy persons, even if they were Communists." [25]

In more recent times, the observer is struck by innumerable statements testifying to a complete lack of anti-religious enthusiasm either in the center or in the provinces.

Chief among the official agencies entrusted with anti-religious action is the Commissariat for Education. However, its practice is rather one of "liquidating" anti-religious activity. It has liquidated a number of anti-religious museums; the publication of anti-religious pictures has been discontinued, and no anti-religious film has been produced since 1938; only one institution for higher anti-religious education has been left, and it is difficult to find students for it.[26]

Special courses for anti-religious propagandists are still offered, but are of little use, for, after graduation, the students remain absolutely inert. No doubt when they chose the anti-religious "specialty" they hit on it almost at random or perhaps they hoped the training would bring them a state subsidy.[27]

Soviet teachers should be professors of atheism. However, when graduates from schools of education are questioned about anti-religious work, they cannot answer, so great is the abandonment of the field. In the students' journal of these schools there was no article on anti-religious work during 1939.[28]

It is easy to understand why, under such circumstances, the graduates of the schools of education, when they are appointed teachers, cannot successfully convert their pupils to an assured and consistent atheism. The journal of the League complains that the majority do not put out any semblance of anti-religious propaganda and that the teachers are apathetic to evidences of gross religious superstition.[29] In April, 1940, the president of the Militant Atheists League complained that anti-religious work in schools was not being furthered by the departments of public education.[30] On May 9, 1940, *Pravda* complained that schools remembered their anti-religious program only at the approach of Easter or Christmas.

At the same time that the Commissariat of Education

was finding its anti-religious policy increasingly ineffective, the Soviet Press was finding the publication of anti-religious propaganda impossible: in 1938, *Trud* published only three anti-religious articles; no article was published by *Uchitelskaya Gazeta, Krasnaya Gazeta,* or *Gudok.* Anti-religious articles in *Krasnaya Gvardya* have fallen to a fifth.[31] Only three posters appeared in the course of the year. Many official publishers refuse even to consider anti-religious manuscripts.[32] In 1940 occasionally local papers published anti-religious notes; but almost without exception these were merely reprints from material received by their offices from the center; this obviously means that they were not much interested.[33]

Among other agencies, the Young Communist League is officially supposed to be extremely active in anti-religious propaganda. At its Tenth Congress, an article was inserted into the statutes according to which the League was required to explain to the youth the dangers of religious superstition and to organize, for that purpose, special circles and lectures. This clause never has been put into effect. Almost no circles have been organized and very few lectures have been given. The press of the League has paid no attention to religion; its special publishing office has not printed anything on it.[34] The languor of the League was stressed at the provincial conference of the Militant Atheists League held in Petrograd in November, 1938, and at the central conference held in Moscow in September, 1940.[35]

Finally, the Trade Unions, comprising all manual and intellectual workers of the Soviet Union, have been assigned officially to anti-religious work. They do nothing. In 1936, an anti-religious campaign was sketched by the central secretariat but was not carried out.[36] In the provinces, many committees of the trade unions have stopped subsidizing the local organizations of the Militant Atheists League. These committees ignore the rise of religious organizations among workers, absences from factories on religious holidays, and membership in church choirs. When asked for the causes of this indifference, the local officers of the trade unions reply that they cannot find any volunteers. It happens sometimes that the few thousand rubles placed at their disposal as an anti-religious budget are not spent, for there is no business.[37]

Of more significance than the lassitude of the individual agencies especially entrusted with the anti-religious banner are symptoms of indifference or even animosity far and wide in the social fabric. It is frequently reported that the anti-religious clubs, erected at great expense opposite churches, are always closed, for no one will attend them, but that churches are full. So-called Red Corners in villages are deserted.[38] When Soviet officials are requested to make a contribution, they respond perfunctorily. Thus, for instance, specialists in agriculture insert anti-religious clichés in their lectures and then continue without further digressions.[39]

Especially significant is the report on a travelling priest who succeeded in performing what is called a "mass baptism" of children of school age. The reaction to this was: "In agreement with the chairman of the collective farm, local teachers declared that they need not interfere, because the new Constitution permitted the believers to perform religious rites. The secretary of the local Party cell declared that baptism was a private affair of the citizens.

On the pretext that he had much more important things to print, the editor of the local paper refused to publish a protest." [40]

Another example is equally illuminating. A lecturer sent to the Donets basin by the Central Committee of the Militant Atheists League reported that the local authorities in general had been hostile to him; he was not provided with living quarters or means of transportation; after delivering thirty lectures, he was sent back to Moscow and not paid. [41]

### 4

The government has never succeeded in establishing "militant atheism." Its secretaries closed churches, molested the clergy, continually parroted stereotyped antireligious tropes, but their bustling never roused enthusiasm. But are not things on the verge of a change? Has not the government succeeded in breeding "new men," and made graduates of Soviet schools advocates of "positive science," as the Communists wrongly call their doctrine and all its derivations? No, things are not on the verge of change, for the government has not succeeded in raising such men: no giants have risen who would recognize nothing but "positive science."

During the last few years, authorities have been alarmed by a substantial spread of the belief in magic. Pupils of the higher grades in grammar schools who no longer attend church or follow religious rites, frequent fortune tellers to learn the grades they will receive at examinations, and some even expect to influence the outcome of the examinations by charms or cryptic formulas. Among the children educated in anti-religious schools absurd practices are often detected; for instance, they think that knots picked up from planks are charms against pain and bad luck; a lock of hair pulled from the head of a successful classmate is believed to bring luck. In an official Soviet paper, we read: "In schools just those children who are absolutely outside of any church influence prove to be the most inclined to the crudest superstitions. They do not believe in God, but they do believe in charms and amulets; they attribute no force to prayer, but they do attribute mystical connotations to meeting a funeral procession or having a book dropped from the school desk. They make magic knots and whisper magic formulas in order to prevent being asked the lesson." [42]

Similar superstitions are frequent among members of the Young Communist League and in general among adolescents. A Soviet paper has recently reported that a young worker wrote a letter to the editor asking if he could recommend a sorcerer to him; young people frequently seek out charms to speed their love affairs. In the Udmurt republic, on the eve of Epiphany, 1940, boys used an old magic hocus-pocus to guess the names of their future brides. Superstition is widespread among miners, sailors, fliers, drivers, and the like, who boast of being atheists.[43]

It is obvious that the struggle against religion has favored this growth of savage fetishism; in any case, a belief in the miraculous and supernatural continues to exist in the minds of so-called atheists. That such cases are not exceptional has many times been acknowledged by the Soviet press. "Many still retain belief in the power of charms and of sorcery and in the interpretation of dreams," wrote *Pravda.* "People think that the young people are free of superstitions," said the *Antireligioznik;* "unfortunately, in actuality, it is not so; many still hold them." [44]

Failure to create a new generation which would be imbued solely with Marxist dogma has probably been a deadly blow to the hopes of Communists who had resolved to exterminate religion. A short time ago Yaroslavsky expostulated: "It is impossible to build up Communism in a society half of which believes in God and the other half fears the devil." [46] An atheist was never nearer to the truth.

## FOOTNOTES TO CHAPTER FOUR

(1) In Soviet Russia, Trade Unions are government agencies which strictly regiment the behavior of workers; membership in them is not compulsory, but outsiders are not given any public employment, and private enterprises are few and insignificant.

(2) N. S. Timasheff, "State and Church in Soviet Russia," *Put* (No. 10), Prague, 1927.

(3) P. 1939, No. 3; U.G., April 4, 1939; K.P., June 5, 1939.

(4) A. 1939, No. 6.

(5) A. 1939, No. 5; B. 1939, No. 14.

(6) P.S. 1939, No. 11.

(7) I., March 10, 1937.

(8) B.M., February 20, 1935.

(9) *Vozrozhdeniye* (*cf.* Chapter III, note 4), April 12, 1935.

(10) A. 1939, No. 2.

(11) K.G., November 15, 1938; A. 1939, No. 1.

(12) A. 1938, No. 2.

(13) B.(m) 1939, No. 5; A. 1939, No. 11.

(14) P., September 22, 1940.

(15) A. 1940, No. 4; 1941, No. 5.

(16) A. 1938, No. 2 and 8–9; 1939, Nos. 1 and 2.

(17) A. 1939, No. 7.

(18) A. 1939, No. 8.

(19) A. 1939, No. 1.

(20) A. 1938, No. 2; 1940, No. 3.

(21) P., September 22, 1940.

(22) A. 1939, No. 2.

(23) A. 1940, Nos. 4 and 8–9; 1941, No. 5.

(24) A. 1938, No. 1.

(25) *Vozrozhdeniye* (*cf.* Chapter III, note 4), March 17, 1928.
(26) L., March 10, 1937; A. 1938, No. 11.
(27) P.S. 1938, No. 7.
(28) U.G., 1939, No. 90.
(29) A. 1939, No. 8.
(30) P., April 26, 1940.
(31) *Trud* is the official paper of the trade unions. *Uchitelskaya Gazeta* is the official paper of the Commissariat for Education. *Gudok* is a paper especially published for factory workers. *Krasnaya Gvardya* is the publishing house of the Young Communist League.
(32) A. 1938, No. 12.
(33) A. 1940, No. 4.
(34) I., March 10, 1937.
(35) A. 1939, No. 1; P., September 22, 1940.
(36) I., March 10, 1937.
(37) T., November 20, 1938; A. 1939, No. 3.
(38) B. 1938, No. 11; K.P., December 23, 1938.
(39) A. 1939, No. 2.
(40) K.P., March 1, 1938.
(41) A. 1939, No. 1.
(42) U.G., October 23, 1938; B. 1938, No. 30; 1939, Nos. 5 and 15.
(43) O.C., August 28, 1937; B.(m) 1938, No. 11; A. 1939, No. 5.
(44) P., August 20, 1939; A. 1940, No. 4.
(45) B. 1939, No. 14.

# CHAPTER FIVE

# The New Religious Policy

I

IN THE SUMMER OF 1939, a few weeks before the signing
of the Nazi-Soviet pact and the outbreak of the second
World War, a note was published in the official organ of
the Militant Atheists League which could not have appeared a few months earlier.[1] The note referred to an
interview by Kallistratos, the Orthodox Patriarch of
Georgia, with a representative of the League. The Patriarch
described as a vigorous old man of seventy-three with mod-
ernist tendencies (a telephone directory was lying on his
desk beside the Bible), tells his visitor that last Easter a
group of young men tramped into the cathedral where he
was conducting divine service and raised a great commo-
tion; this went on for some fifteen minutes until they
grew tired and left. The representative replies that such
behavior is strongly condemned by the League. The
Patriarch tells then of another case: he says that a few
days before he had met two well dressed girls who deliberately turned the other way when they saw that a priest
was going to pass by them.[2] The interviewer says that the
girls, if atheists at all, were very poor ones. Then the Patriarch explains his interpretation of the future: in his
opinion, there will be a revival of religion and it will fuse
with Communism, for the Communist ideal does not contra-

dict Christian doctrine.[3] The editor of the paper, the chief of the League, added a note to the article, saying that the views of Patriarch Kallistratos were widespread among the Russian clergy and the people.

The same issue prints an "open letter" to the editor from an "old man in Leningrad." Objecting to an article published in an earlier issue, the "old man" says that people have indeed preserved many prejudices and superstitions, but that they also have much common sense; they realize that leniency in the struggle against religion today is necessary for the people, and not only for the people, but also for the government in order to encourage morality and to give the younger generation a solid education; it would be harmful to increase religious oppression; a conference of the clergy should be convoked and their aid solicited to draw up a statute which would serve common interests. No comment was made on this letter which, it must again be stressed, appeared in the official journal of the League.

These facts testify to a highly complex situation. The struggle against religion has not been stopped in Russia, as the very existence of the Militant Atheists League indicates; but it has taken a new form of partial compromise, for religion has proved to be the most tenacious and indestructible of all the survivals from pre-revolutionary Russia.

2

Compromise with religion runs counter to the fundamental principles of Marxism as they have been consistently interpreted and taught in the course of the Soviet rule. These principles are unchangeable but their interpretation and application may vary. A new version was formulated at the very beginning of the New Religious Policy, for Communism is an ideocracy, that is, the rule of a system of ideas, externalized and faithfully executed by those in power. The new version demonstrated that implacable warfare with Christianity was not necessary because Christianity had not always been a reactionary force as was at first supposed by the Marxist agitators. This thesis had to be developed: (1) in regard to Christianity in general, and (2) specifically in regard to the role of Christianity in Russia.

An appropriate explication of the first part of the new thesis was reached after a thorough discussion of the problem during three joint sessions of the Historical Institute of the Academy of Sciences and of the Central Committee of the Militant Atheists League, held December 12, 16, and 22, 1938. A paper elaborated by Professor Ranovich, the subject of discussion, was finally endorsed by both bodies. Its main propositions were as follows:

The Communist Party has been in error about the origin of Christianity. Two theories had prevailed: Professor Wipper's, to whom Christianity had been from the beginning a religion of exploiters, and Kautsky's, to whom Christianity was an escape from misery, primarily a religion of slaves and freedmen. Actually, Christianity is an opiate for the people, as every religion is; but it must be explained why it has proved to be the most successful. The answer is that Christianity was a substantially new religious movement. It did not allow racial or national discrimination. It anticipated new forms of marriage. It recognized the dignity of the "abstract man" and proclaimed the equality of men independently of their social status. Among early Christians, revolt against the existing social order was the rule. Early communities were democratic, and their spirit was revolutionary. Later on, Christianity was subjected to many changes, but still preserved its ideals of human dignity and universalism. The progressive role Christianity has played, in comparison with other religions, is undeniable: it introduced new ideas, a basis on which a new society could be built.[4]

A few months later, Ranovich's propositions ratified by the Militant Atheists League appeared in a circular addressed to the propagandists of atheism. "Christianity should not be identified with capitalism. Early Christians were not rich, and they did not pay much attention to wealth. Christianity should not be identified with other religions: for it is a cult of the 'abstract man' and emphasizes his ideal properties. The beneficial role Christianity played in the development of family relations should not be denied, for it helped to establish monogamy. Christianity has contributed to the improvement of folkways and customs; it has eliminated bloody and orgiastic rites; it insisted on the abolition of harmful customs such as fights between gladiators and the coursing of men by beasts in the circus." [5]

For the second part of the new thesis, the Communist leaders had only to return to ideas which had been formulated during the incident of Borodin's *Knights* (see above Chapter II, section 6). In 1939, both the weekly and the monthly organs of the Militant Atheists League discussed the Christianization of Russia with unmistakable mellowness. "It would be wrong to think," wrote Oleschuk in the *Antireligioznik,* "that everything connected with religion is necessarily reactionary, because religion in itself is reactionary. It is especially wrong to think that the Christianization of Russia was a reactionary step, as, unfortunately, has been asserted in our anti-religious activity" . . . "The Christianization of Russia by Prince Vladimir," wrote the *Bezbozhnik,* "certainly was a progressive act. Christianity struggled against slavery and blood feuds; it condemned the sale of Christians into slavery and fostered the replacement of slavery by the milder institution of serfdom; Christianity favored the advance of culture and laid the foundation of Russian art and literature." [6]

About the same time the idea was circulated that "it was wrong to put on the black list events and personalities only because they were in some manner connected with the Church." Grand Duke Alexander Nevsky was recalled who, in the thirteenth century, successfully protected Russia against the invasion of Germans and Swedes. "Despite the fact that Alexander Nevsky is considered a saint by the Orthodox Church and that many churches and monasteries have been dedicated to him, atheists have to avoid any defamation of his memory; they must remember that he is a beloved hero of the people and that he merited the gratitude of later generations by his patriotism and military prowess. The Church canonized him in consideration of the love of the people; the Militant Atheists League has failed to pursue an equally wise policy." [7]

A film, produced about that time, provoked enlightening criticism: "In the film 'Alexander Nevsky' the clergy is almost altogether absent. There is, however, no reason to be afraid of objectively showing the role of the Church in Russian history. Anti-religious propaganda is permissible in films of this kind; however, it must be directed not against the Orthodox clergy, but against Catholic monks and the Roman Pope." [8]

The instructions concerning the Orthodox clergy were not confined to paper: in the film "Suvorov," the famous Russian general is shown constantly making the sign of the cross, and other religious symbols are in evidence.

The recognition of positive values incorporated in Christianity and in Christian institutions did not stop at this point. Discussing the possibility and desirability of the united action of Communist and Catholic workers in Western democracies, the Atheists League acknowledged that the teaching of the Gospel of love for one's neighbor and fraternity was accepted by all workmen. About that time, it was said that Stalin had become a revolutionist because, in the Tiflis seminary where he studied, he was disgusted with the fact that millions of men were not permitted to believe as they wished.[9]

The new version of the Marxist view of religion was to be explained to all involved. One possibility was to revise statements in the fundamental works of Communism, for such revisions were becoming more and more common in other fields. Thus, for instance, it was said that Marx and Lenin could not have foreseen the peculiar position of "one socialist country encircled by capitalist states" nor the many changes produced by the technical advance of the last decades, and the genesis of new military problems.[10]

It was, however, impossible to use this formula for religion. Therefore, less drastic measures were selected which were somewhat contradictory, but in a dictatorship this did not matter.

The first vindication of Communist policy was pure falsehood. It was asserted that the Party had always acted according to the principles emphasized in 1939. "We frequently hear," stated one of the papers of the Militant Atheists League, "that believers and non-believers are two hostile camps which necessarily must struggle against one another. This is an insidious lie, discrediting to the antireligious movement. We cannot stop the struggle against religion for we have never fought it" . . . "the Communist Party has always struggled on two fronts: first, against those who considered that religion was a private affair of the citizens, and second, against those who exaggerated its importance and demanded its immediate extermination by administrative measures." [11] Obviously the Party, or, more exactly, its leadership, had intended "to exterminate religion by administrative measures," when it launched the attacks of 1922, 1929, and 1937. No one could have forgotten it; the new directions meant that, in 1939, everyone was ordered to wink at the oppression of those terrible years.

The second justification was a declaration that the new policy was the true interpretation of Marxism, whereas the old policy had been a misconception, not on the part of the leadership, which was infallible, but of the Militant Atheists League and local Communists. This time, in contrast to 1930, Yaroslavsky had to swallow many of his own ironical words [12] and even to publish qualifications in papers of the League. Since the beginning of 1939, it has often been stressed that the enforcement of the anti-religious policy during elections to the Supreme Soviet had been overdone. Yaroslavsky's aide, Oleschuk, wrote: "Our League has committed many blunders in regard to Christianity. Marxist atheists have assumed the policy of bourgeois atheists. They denied Christianity in general without taking into consideration special circumstances. Marxist atheists must exercise a concrete approach and must realize that the Church has not always been a harmful influence." [13]

It was admitted that the League had erred in history and theory. There had been an utter failure to understand the historical importance of the Christianization of Russia and of the canonization of national heroes. The League was accused of having acted on the supposition that the strength of religion came from the ignorance of the masses and their betrayal by the priests. This was the repetition of an obvious mistake made by bourgeois atheists and incompatible with the doctrine of Lenin and Stalin who insisted that religion was rooted in social conditions.[14] To reinforce the historical argument the Communists have skillfully resorted to the policy of worshipping national heroes. Discussing the methods of Peter the Great, the reformer of Russia, they said that his religious policy was worthy of imitation, for he understood that not all the clergy resisted his reforms, but only the reactionary minority.[15] If Peter the Great made distinctions, why should not Communists make similar ones? Such was the novel rationalization.

A third statement of policy probably corresponded to facts more closely than the others. Bluntly stated, it was the definition of Communist policy as opportunism, which at certain times requires the sacrifice of principles to political expedience. Naturally, such ideas were adroitly couched in Marxist terminology. Early in 1939, it was declared that anti-religious propaganda was to be co-ordinated with the exigencies of class struggle; consequently, the activity of the Atheists League had to be subordinated to other, more primary, political problems. A few months later, in discussing the functions of the League, its journal explained that it was the duty of every Marxist to evaluate the particular situation at any given time and place. After the annexation of Eastern Poland, Militant Atheists were once more reminded that Lenin and Stalin rebuked those Communists who considered that the struggle against religion was in all circumstances necessary; this struggle had to be subordinated to general policy. In 1939 general policy forced the Soviet government to permit citizens to profess any religion they pleased, above all to tolerate those national and religious groups which previously had been persecuted.[16]

This blatant opportunism provoked misunderstanding and dissatisfaction among the local Communists, especially when "Common Front" became the official slogan abroad. So long as this policy was enforced, friendly gestures were made by Communist leaders towards "the masses of Catholic believers," in distinction to the "princes of the Church" because, in these masses, the Communist government hoped to find allies against Fascism. This attitude was hardly compatible with simultaneous developments within Russia, characterized by the fierce persecution of 1937-38, and produced almost a revolt among Communists working in the local Party organizations. They criticized the inconsistency of the government's religious policy; it was styled a hypocritical combination of atheism for Russia and friendliness towards Christians outside the country. The official rejoinder was that, according to the instructions of

the Communist International, Communist parties outside
had to unite believers in a common front against Fascism,
whose reactionary anti-religious policy was an Achilles' heel.
But the section of the Comintern in Russia (the Union
Communist Party) had to act under completely different
conditions; it had to regard religion as a combination of
sentiments and views which were essentially hostile to Communism. In both cases the struggle against religion was
subordinated to the class struggle; the inconsistency seized
upon by opponents was merely the result of the application
of dialectical materialism to dissimilar exigencies.[17] These
explanations seem never to have completely convinced the
local Communists, and only the reconciliation of the religious policy within Russia with that elsewhere helped
them to find a way through. The situation, of course,
changed again when the policy of the Common Front was
abandoned after the transaction with Hitler. New explanations were invented and imposed on the local Communists
(see below, section 5).

3

Actions accompanied these theoretical discussions and
interpretations. First of all, a tendency has been accelerated
which originated during the lull between the second and
the third frontal attack and which was at least partially
maintained during the third. This was to refuse to permit
acts of direct violence against the masses of believers,
although persecution of the clergy continued.

The following events of the latter part of 1937 may be
considered as precedents: the Committee of the Communist
Party of the province of Ivanovo (north of Moscow) ex-

pelled from the Party and removed from his position the
editor of the paper in Vichuga (near Yaroslavl) for ad-
vocating the forcible closing of churches; the action was
taken because Moscow warned the Ivanovo authorities that
such an attitude was helpful to the enemy. Similar occur-
rences were reported in the province of Orel. When the
Smolensk province Party secretaries invited the people at
electoral meetings to sign petitions for the wholesale closing
of churches, *Pravda* declared this to be outright provoca-
tion, and demanded the punishment of those responsible.[18]

In 1939, this tendency gained momentum. Soviet agencies
were directed to stop all attempts to liquidate religion. Sub-
sequently it was decreed that any attempt to combat religion by administrative measures, especially by the closing
of churches, was to be discontinued. Atheists must be careful to avoid offending the religious sentiments of the believers, and pioneers were admonished to refrain from
ridiculing Christian children in schools. Still later, the Militant Atheists League was entrusted with the task of opposing the attempts of other agencies to suppress religion by
administrative measures.[19] Militant Atheists checking anti-
religious outbursts! Is this not an almost unimaginable
irony of Providence?

The new instructions have been obeyed, and violators
are severely reprimanded or even punished. Around Easter
in 1939, in a suburb of Moscow, a few enthusiastic members of the Militant Atheists League gathered children and
urged them to make a great hullabaloo during divine service. The children obeyed and thereby, commented the
organ of the League, "caused immense harm to the Soviet
government." In a number of villages around Tula and

Riazan, the same journal reported, icons and sacred vessels taken from closed churches were made objects of public derision. The result was not a decrease in religious sentiment, but an increase in anti-Soviet feeling. Several members of the Yaroslavl Party organization were indicted for organizing a "hooligan raid" at Easter on a village church. One was sentenced to eighteen months in prison, others from six months to a year of compulsory labor without imprisonment. Commenting on this trial, *Pravda* wrote: "The trial in Yaroslavl proved that in the USSR there is freedom of worship. But the trial produced also detrimental effects: rumors were spread that the atheists had been tried because the Communist government needed the support of religion." [20] The interview with the Patriarch of Georgia, reported in Section 1, also must be interpreted as a form of indemnity inflicted on atheists for activities which for a long time had been recommended by the government but were no longer in favor.

Trials against "religionists" were stopped. The last trial of this kind was reported from the remote Buryat-Mongolian Republic (eastern Siberia) where instructions are fully digested only months after they have been issued in Moscow: in April, 1939, a group of counter-revolutionists were tried there; "kulaks" and clergy were involved; the alleged conspiracy of the defendants was to overthrow the Soviet government with the help of Japan.[21]

Anti-religious propaganda became milder and somewhat more respectful. Atheists were warned not to nettle believers. Christianity was to be treated with the veneration due to its historical role. Propagandists were no longer to show contempt for the word "Church." [22]

Very revealing is an instruction published in 1940. The fact that in the USSR many people continue to pray means that they are dissatisfied with the material and moral conditions of their existence. That is the point at which the activity of the League should be leveled: the League should explain to the workers that their conditions are satisfactory.[23]

Equally descriptive of the new forms of anti-religious propaganda have been two speeches of Kalinin, the President of the Supreme Soviet of the USSR. At a teachers' conference, he said that the teaching of Marxism should no longer be understood as the teaching of the Marxist doctrine. Education in the Marxist spirit should mean the inculcation of love for the socialist fatherland, friendship, comradeship, humanism, honesty and cooperation in work; of course, respect for the Soviet government and love for Comrade Stalin should not be forgotten. On another occasion he said that it was not enough to destroy religion; it was necessary to replace it by something else, and Lenin had said that in the society of the future, the theater would play the role formerly held by religion.[24] Statements of a remarkable modesty when set against the first boasts that religion would wither away under the invincible rays of Marxist truth!

Further concessions to the Orthodox manner of life were made, in themselves small but adding up to an impressive total. Artisans of the townships of Mstera and Palekha (near Nizhni Novgorod, now Gorki) who for generations had been famous icon painters were permitted to work on the restoration of old icons. State drugstores are now selling oil for lamps to burn before icons. Removing an icon from a room against the desire of the head of the family has been declared to be an unlawful violation of religious freedom, a measure which does not sap, but rather invigorates religious sentiment. The practice of giving children Christian names is no longer objected to "because many revolutionists had such names." It is now permissible to celebrate Easter night with noisy festivity.[25]

Even more momentous is the fact that when, under the pressure of circumstances, the Soviet government had to abandon the six-day week and to return to the usual one, Sunday was made the rest day. When this decree was about to be issued, the atheist leaders urged that Monday or Wednesday take the place of Sunday. The protest was disregarded, and Professor Nikolsky was commissioned to write an article for the official paper of the League explaining that no other day would be convenient as a holiday since the majority of the nation, *i.e.*, people living in the villages, insisted on observing Sunday and that a discrepancy between town and country would be unthinkable.[26]

Besides the main platform of mitigated persecution, a few secondary trends can be read into the New Religious Policy. First, the usefulness of religion as the guardian of morality seems to have been grasped by those in power. Yaroslavsky has stated that, on this point, the Militant Atheists League was far behind the Church; and, in the journal of which he is the editor, he published, without comment, a letter which emphasized the moral role of religion (see above, section 1). The same journal has published numerous reports in which the discreditable behavior of Communist youth is contrasted with the orderly behavior of those who adhered to the old tradition. This is the more important as moral disorganization has gradually been recognized by the rulers as disastrous to the fulfillment of social and technical ends. It is probable that, in 1939, the elevation of religion to a more or less tolerable status was considered by the Communist rulers as a means of moral stabilization. But objections to such a plan must have been formidable, and nothing of importance was done.

Second, during the last few years there has been a tendency to focus persecution on the Roman Catholic Church. The comments on the Alexander Nevsky film (see above, section 2) are symptomatic, as well as the discussion of the policy to be followed in the provinces annexed from Poland (see below, section 5): in both cases, the Catholic clergy has been declared *the* enemy. And deeds bear out words: fewer than a dozen Catholic priests are known to live at liberty in the Soviet State, and hundreds are imprisoned, a situation that does not exist for the clergy of other religious groups. These facts can be easily explained: the restoration of the old alliance between the State and the Orthodox Church is only a remote possibility, but the Communists have gradually realized that the national Church of Russia whose head is in captivity is much less dangerous for them than the international organization of Catholicism.

Third, the Communist rulers have begun to see that it was easier to keep religion within limits when it was under the jurisdiction of a well organized and centralized Church, than to try to curtail the activities of thousands of local sects or of the travelling priests (Chapter III, section 3). The realization of this has probably induced the Communist government to concede that it is preferable to canalize religion (which they now know cannot be destroyed) within a visible and instituted Church. Consequently, in an almost imperceptible manner, throughout the years of the New Religious Policy, "sects" have been treated with less leniency than the Orthodox Church, whereas in earlier years the attitude of the Communist rulers of Russia had been the reverse.

As the New Religious Policy had been in operation for only about two and a half years when the Russo-German war broke out, the three tendencies were not sufficiently crystallized to permit definite judgment, and it would be pure guesswork to discuss what would have been the outcome, if a completely new situation had not arisen as the result of the war.

## 4

The New Religious Policy, both in its main tendency and its details, indicates a substantial change in the strategy of the government. However, the extent should not be exaggerated. The government has not been converted and continues to consider atheism as the official doctrine of the State. In the Summer of 1939, when the new policy was in full swing, members of the Party and of the Young Communist League were reminded that they would be expelled from the Party or the League if they performed any religious rite; this had been Stalin's proclamation in 1927, and it was said to be still valid, since such rites are directly opposed to the *raison d'être* of the two organizations.

There is, in the midst of the Soviet population, another group whose members are not allowed to believe or to adhere to any kind of idealistic philosophy. These are the scientists. Every Soviet scientist, as has been said, must study dialectics; therefore, unlike the bourgeois scientist, his religious whimsies cannot be explained away as a lack of knowledge. Soviet scientists must not only be atheists, but must also take an active part in the war against religion. The greatest of the Russian scientists of our day, Pavlov, was reproached in an article published after his death for having remained tainted with pietism and for having scolded the Communist government for its anti-religious vandalism. This was explained by his old age and was commented on as an anomaly.[28]

Furthermore, although anti-religious propaganda has been revised it has received rather increased importance because other methods of pressure have been discontinued. In the Summer of 1939, *Pravda* issued an energetic reminder of the necessity for combating religion: "Many still adhere to the rites and superstitions of the old Church, continue to believe in religious doctrines, in the power of charms, sorcery and the interpretation of dreams. The existence of such a religious ideology offers a fruitful field for the activity of the enemies of the people, especially among the peasantry." [29] It is noteworthy that belief and superstition are confused. As has already been shown (Chapter IV), the Communist government knows that this association is false: it is not those who continue to believe in God, but the converts to atheism who are inclined to believe in magic. But, for reasons of political expediency, the Communist paper asserts the opposite; the game is obviously to make religion ridiculous, by identifying it with such nonsense as charms or sorcery. This is, incidentally, one of the conventional lines in anti-religious propaganda.

As religion still exists and still is a danger, it must be fought. "In the USSR there is complete freedom of religion," say the atheists in their journal. "But we demand that the Soviet State conduct anti-religious propaganda. Certainly, not by administrative measures, but by ideological methods, through speeches, the press, the school, the theater, the club, the radio." [30]

The weakness of the anti-religious effort is well known to the government (see Chapter IV); but could not this effort be improved? Numerous acts and declarations for reform may be selected from the year 1940. On February 27, the Commissariat of Education issued instructions for the improvement of anti-religious work in schools. Once more, it was acknowledged that in schools, anti-religious training was very poorly organized; special reading on anti-religious themes seemed to be unknown, excursions to anti-religious museums very rare. Consequently, schools were once more ordered to pay more attention to anti-religious propaganda; the headmasters were advised to request help from pioneers and the Young Communist League; special anti-religious circles were to be organized for the parents.[31]

On April 25, 1940, at a meeting of the Presidium of the Militant Atheists League, Yaroslavsky complained that anti-religious work in schools was still half-hearted. A special committee for the advancement of anti-religious work among children was established. On May 9, 1940, *Pravda* opened a campaign for the founding of more schools for training propagandists of atheism. It complained, as we have already seen, that many schools took up anti-religious work only at the approach of Easter and Christmas.[32]

After the annexation of the Baltic States, Yaroslavsky discussed the prospects of atheism in these areas. Despite the fact that the Soviet conquest has been short-lived, it is worth while quoting his statements, as they give insight into the contemporary religious policy of the Communist government.

"Since 22 years have not been enough to liquidate the Church in the USSR, we shall have many difficulties in extirpating the remains of religious prejudices in the Baltic countries. One of the reasons is that many people consider anti-religious propaganda no longer necessary. This opinion is false. Anti-religious propaganda is one of the essential aspects of Communist propaganda and must be carried out by a special organization. The reproach which might be made against the atheists is that they have not been able to offer the people moral standards for their life. Religion answered moral questions in its way." [33]

Providing people with moral standards of Communist origin is one of the aims of reorganized propaganda. Explaining to them that their life is beautiful is another (see above, section 2). A third is the inculcation of the idea that religion is merely an historical phenomenon and therefore will cease to exist, if properly handled. This last point is discussed in the weekly paper of the Militant Atheists League: "Some members of the Party have reached the desperate solution that religious sentiment is inborn and cannot be eliminated. This is a wrong idea. Quite primitive tribes have no religion, which appears in the medium grade of savagery. In capitalist society religion is necessary as a means of exploitation; in Socialist society it is useless just as it was in primitive society, and it is even detrimental for it inculcates in men ideas opposed to those of Marx, Lenin, and Stalin." [34]

There are even symptoms of a partial revision of the relatively liberal interpretations made in the beginning of the period of the New Religious Policy. In a lecture delivered on October 10, 1940, Yaroslavsky's aide, Oleschuk, declared that it was incorrect to ascribe progressive tendencies to Christianity as such, that it had played a progressive role only in specific epochs, and that any attempt to find a compromise between Christianity and Communism was counter-revolutionary. [35]

On the other hand, despite the inauguration of the New Religious Policy, religious propaganda continues to be illegal. No religious press is permitted; since 1927, no reprints of the Bible have been made. No one is permitted to preach religion in open meetings. Religious instruction may be given only by parents to their children and not too openly. Nothing resembling Sunday schools or Bible classes is permissible in the atheist state. [36]

Finally, compensation for the destructive measures of the earlier periods has not been made. The legal status of the parishes, the dioceses and the national Churches is the same as it was in 1918, i.e., precarious toleration. The Greek Orthodox Church has not been permitted to convoke a National Council nor to elect a Patriarch. Churches closed by force have not been reopened; anti-religious museums and schools of anti-religious education continue to exist, although in smaller numbers than ten years ago. [37] Bishops and priests imprisoned or confined to concentration camps have not been released.

The situation is not clear in regard to discrimination

against believers. A decrease in its intensity was already noticeable in 1935–36 (see above Chapter II, section 6); and the instructions issued under the New Religious Policy explicitly prohibit it.[38] However, since there never was any official discrimination against laymen, the time which has elapsed since the inauguration of the new policy is not yet sufficient to make a final judgment on the new practice. But the compulsory atheism imposed on the ruling group and the scientists shows that, in any case, the believers have no access to the higher social positions.

### 5

Since the New Religious Policy has never been officially formulated as a definite program, its nature must be tested by applications to new problems which have arisen since its inauguration. The check is the more conclusive as there exists information emanating from two independent sources —official Soviet declarations and summaries of clandestine reports published by highly reliable agencies.

The occupation of Eastern Poland by Soviet troops seems to have been accompanied by the excesses characteristic of the first days of Communism; the "liquidation" of large numbers of priests, both Greek Orthodox and Roman Catholic, has been acknowledged, and, for a while, in the newly acquired provinces, the sort of propaganda used around 1930 was resumed. "Everything that happened in Russia during the Revolution reappeared," wrote the *Bezbozhnik*. "The Catholic priests with arms in hands tried to save the capitalist enslavement of workers." [39]

However, very soon the Communist government came

to the conclusion that the New Religious Policy should be applied in the newly acquired lands. Acting Patriarch Sergius was permitted to appoint a number of bishops, and government spokesmen made a number of significant statements.

Mikhailov, the head of the Young Communist League, said that both the Soviet and the Nazi States were opposed to Christian ideology and had common enemies, chief of whom were the Catholic clergy. The two governments must swap information and act together, especially after the partition of Poland. However, the cooperation was limited. The Communist Party fought religion because it was opposed to materialism and not because of the racialism which determined Nazi activities but was unacceptable to the Soviet. Moreover, the Communists could not follow the Nazi policy on the Orthodox Church in Poland; for the Communists were acting in conformity with the Stalin Constitution: religious worship was permissible so long as religious organizations recognized the nature of the new order in Russia and did not oppose it.[40]

On February 5, 1940, *Izvestia* spoke of "counter-revolutionary rumors of the coming religious persecution in Western White Russia and Western Ukraine," rumors which had impressed a number of "class unconscious workers." Actually no anti-religious measures were contemplated, and Party Leaders were told to deny them and to disseminate correct information among the local inhabitants. A few days later, the head of the Militant Atheists League officially declared that no cells of the League would be organized in the newly annexed provinces, despite the fact that there the clergy were influential.

The chief task of the day was to expose the numerous lies of enemies of the Soviet. The anti-religious activity in these provinces was to be limited to the organization of anti-religious conferences and to the education of the masses.[41]

On August 21, 1940, a decree on agrarian reform was issued in Lithuania, according to which every parish priest was to be granted 3 ha. (about 8.1 acres) of arable land, even if his parish had not previously owned any land. Priests who had previously owned land were to be allowed as much as 30 ha. (about 81 acres), just as the peasants.[42]

From a non-Soviet source comes the following interesting statement by Cardinal Hlond of Poland: "The policy adopted [by Communists in Eastern Poland] is to avoid massacres and other barbaric methods in favor of others, more subtle and efficient, already tested by experience. As a consequence, the Russians seek to undermine the importance of the Church, to degrade the clergy and, above all, to educate the youth to atheism and communism. For this reason, there are no organized massacres of priests; the few cases so far recorded were due to local Communists. To impoverish the clergy, the Commissariat of Internal Affairs confiscated all church property and deprived the priests of their revenue, forcing them to beg for their living. At the same time it disorganized dioceses and forbade bishops to attend to their administration and to visit the parishes. The propaganda for atheism is done through slogans coming from Moscow. It is not so gross as in the early years of the Soviet regime. Atheism is preached scientifically. Repugnant blasphemy has been replaced by skillful skepticism which is instilled especially into the children. The banning of religion from schools is applied gradually. The cross is, in some cases, permitted to remain in school rooms, but it must be placed between portraits of Lenin and Stalin." [43]

From the Baltic countries, this information has reached the Swedish paper *Kyrkor under Korset* (Church under the Cross): "The priests are still at work, but their economic situation is growing more and more difficult. The ministers marry, baptize and bury people unhindered as they used to do. State officials have been ordered to stay away from church and not to ask ministers for any official services. The Roman Catholic priests are reported to be standing fast. They continue to wear their official dress. Many of them, like the clergy of other confessions, have learned a craft so as to maintain themselves more easily. One of the first things to be transformed is the school system and education in general. There is no longer any such thing as a Christian school. Hundreds of school teachers have been dismissed; in their place students are being appointed after a course of instruction in Communism." [44]

This information shows that, in the newly annexed provinces, the policy of the Soviet government has been that of co-ordination, or of gradual adjustment to the conditions prevailing in the old provinces since the enactment of the New Religious Policy. It once more proves that the limits of the change effected by this policy are relatively narrow. The Church organization is still prevented from functioning. Anti-religious education continues to dominate. What is in abeyance are outright persecution and open blasphemy.

6

Finally, in June, 1941, war broke out. Information about events since then is scanty, and any judgment of the situation must be made with great caution.

The first Sunday after the beginning of hostilities, Acting Patriarch Sergius conducted a high mass at his cathedral, assisted by twenty-six priests. Prayers were offered for the victory of Soviet troops. Twelve thousand worshippers crowded the old cathedral and several thousands overflowed the yard. At the same time, the Acting Patriarch sent a message to all churches in the Soviet Union, enjoining prayers and patriotic efforts to defeat what he called the enemy of Russia and of humanity. "The Orthodox Church," he wrote, "always has shared the nation's fate. It always has carried its burdens and cherished its successes. We will not desert the nation now. Christ's Church blesses all Orthodox members defending the Fatherland's sacred borders. God will grant victory." [45] The message was not ignored: about the end of December, 1941, the Archbishop of Samara (Kuibysheff) told a representative of the Associated Press that, throughout the country, prayers for the victory of the Russian armies were sung at high mass. Many soldiers in uniform or in plain clothes attended the services. In his opinion, the Russian nation has been entrusted by God with the task of restoring the mental balance of the enemy and of preserving Western Europe from Hitler who has invented his own god.[46]

On August 21, 1941, the Moscow radio called upon "all God-loving inhabitants of the occupied countries" to rise in defense of their religious freedom. It charged the German regime with menacing "the very existence of Christianity and seeking the overthrow of Christ the King, to install instead the myth of the Twentieth Century of Alfred Rosenberg." [47]

One month later, the publication of *Bezbozhnik,* the weekly of the Militant Atheists League, was discontinued: also in a few days, the *Antireligioznik,* the League's monthly.[48] Gradually, "anti-religious voices have been completely silenced, and the flood of literature once devoted to this subject has ceased." [49] Although it was officially stated that the suspension had been ordered to conserve paper, it would be correct to point out that this is an indication of a more liberal attitude toward worship and a toning down of the attacks on the clergy and believers. Nor would it be going too far to say that anything pleasing to the United States and Britain is looked on with favor, and that American diplomats have informed the Soviet government that President Roosevelt himself was interested and would be delighted to see further generosity in the interpretation of Stalin's Constitution. The suspension of the anti-religious publications might be thought of as a response to the friendly pressure of the Allies.[50] In any case, on November 18, at a banquet in honor of American and British guests, Stalin said: "May God help President Roosevelt in his task," words which would have been inconceivable a few months earlier.[51]

During the Russian offensive which began on December 7, 1941, Russian papers complained that retreating German armies had pillaged and burned celebrated churches and monasteries—that so many had been desecrated in peacetime by the Communists was not mentioned.[52] For the convenience of those attending Easter midnight services, the curfew was lifted in Moscow, and naturally, as reported from Russia, at these services Moscow's churches were full.[53]

According to other information, however, in March, 1941, in the Baltic countries, religion was already under fire. "A number of religious associations were dissolved as being inimical to the State, and their members, including many ministers, have been arrested as enemies of the people. Churches have been closed, monasteries dissolved, and the liquidation of the clergy accelerated. An anti-religious reign of terror has begun in the Baltic area." [54]

According to the same source, "with the outbreak of war there was an intensification rather than diminution of anti-religious activity." Acts of direct attack, among them the execution by retreating Communists of Bishop Simeon of Kremenets and of four hundred churchgoers, have been reported to Russian *émigré* groups.

From among the opposing tendencies, that of leniency seems to have prevailed. According to the latest reports, it is now realized (by the Soviet government) that "religious faith is part and parcel of the national Russian make-up." [55] Consequently, at least for the duration of the war, religion must be given some consideration. American diplomats were told that no change in law was contemplated, but some laxity in its enforcement had become the dominant note.[56] The church has earned this tolerance. "Particularly in the occupied regions priests and believers have stoutly resisted German attempts to use them politically in an anti-Soviet sense. A story is told of a high personage who while decorating guerrillas stepped before a shaggy-headed and bearded hero and said kindly, 'But you know you ought to have your hair cut.' The reply was, 'But I am not allowed to; I am a priest.' " [57]

### 7

From war adjustments and from incidents observable in the annexed provinces, we may summarize the results of the New Religious Policy by two comparisons:

If the present situation is compared with the truly Neronian atrocities of 1937–38, the amelioration is glaring and must be so felt by those involved; they may come out of the catacombs into the fresh air and need not fear that deadly recriminations will follow their declarations of faith; they may also be assured that there will be no gross interference with worship; and they no longer expect, every day, announcements of the arrest of bishops and priests or of the demolition of churches.

But if this is compared with religious freedom as it is understood in America, the contrast is striking: religion is tolerated, but it is not permitted to function according to its rights; not only is no one allowed to propagate religion, that is, to convert pagans, but no one is even permitted to refute openly the insults of atheism.

In the USSR, State and Church are officially separated. In actuality, the State is separated from Christianity but is closely connected with the pseudo-Church of anti-Christianity: the leaders of the Communist State are still the prophets and the leaders of Militant Atheism. In this, the New Religious Policy has changed nothing.

## FOOTNOTES TO CHAPTER FIVE

(1) B. 1939, No. 21.

(2) According to a curious Russian superstition, to meet a clergy-man is a bad omen.

(3) Speaking of a possible fusion of religion and Communism, the Patriarch obviously had in mind that the meaning of Communism could be narrowed to that of a particular form of production and distribution, with the elimination of the philosophical premises given to it by Marx.

(4) A. 1939, No. 1.

(5) A. 1939, No. 4.

(6) A. 1939, No. 5; B. 1939, Nos. 4 and 5.

(7) A. 1939, Nos. 5 and 6.

(8) B.(m) 1938, No. 12.

(9) A. 1939, No. 4; B.(m) 1939, No. 6.

(10) K.G., November 26 and 27, 1938; U.G., April 17, 1939; *Bolshevik,* 1939, No. 1; *Propaganda i agitatsia,* 1939, No. 2; P., June 14, 1939.

(11) A. 1939, Nos. 1 and 5.

(12) In 1933, he bluntly asserted that Christianity had fostered slavery (*Religion in USSR,* in Russian, pp. 30–33).

(13) A. 1939, Nos. 1 and 6.

(14) P., March 20, 1940.

(15) A. 1939, No. 7.

(16) B. 1939, No. 3; B.(m) 1939, No. 8.

(17) A. 1939, Nos. 2 and 5.

(18) P., October 25, and November 29, 1937.

(19) B. 1939, Nos. 3, 9, and 12.

(20) P., July 1, 1939; B. 1939, No. 14.

(21) *Buryato-Mongolskaya Pravda,* April 18, 1939.

(22) A. 1939, No. 4.

(23) P., March 20, 1940.

(24) K.P., April 11, 1939; U.G., July 13, 1939.

(25) B. 1939, Nos. 10, 14, and 23; A. 1939, No. 9. It is also significant that prohibition of interference with Paschal celebrations was applied to Hebrews also whose religion was not protected by the new interpretation of Christianity. About the same time the Commissariat of Justice explained that the persecution of mullahs and rabbis for performing circumcision was illegal; from the report it appears that formerly they had been prosecuted for the violation of the article of the criminal code on abortion!

(26) *The Tablet* (London), February 15, 1941.

(27) B. 1939, No. 15.

(28) B. 1939, Nos. 4 and 6. Pavlov is reported to have said: "What evil do you see in the ringing of the church bells? They could remind us of our childhood and of its happiness. Well, in order to manifest my dissatisfaction, I will attend at Holy Mass."

(29) P., August 20, 1939.

(30) A. 1939, No. 4.

(31) A. 1940, No. 4. It may be asserted that this instruction did not produce any substantial change. The Young Communist League and the Pioneers do not care for anti-religious work (as has been shown in Chapter IV); in any case, the passive resistance of schools seems to have remained unshaken; according to A. 1940, No. 7, the instruction of February 27 has not reached any agency below the provincial boards of education; schools and teachers do not know of its existence.

(32) P., April 26, and May 9, 1940.

(33) B. 1940, No. 4.

(34) B. 1939, No. 5.

(35) A. 1940, No. 12.

(36) Cf. President Roosevelt's statement reported to the N. Y. Times, October 1, 1941.

(37) In 1941, there existed two principal museums (in Moscow and Leningrad), 17 republican and 27 provincial museums (A. 1941, No. 4).

(38) B.(m) 1939, No. 8.

(39) B. 1939, No. 29.

(40) Poslednya Novosti (published in Russian, in Paris), January 21, 1941. The Soviet papers which published the original report were unavailable.

(41) I., February 5, 1940; B. 1940, No. 4.

(42) I. F. Trainin, "The Constitutions of the new Soviet Republics" (in Russian), Vestnik Akademii Nauk, 1940, No. 10–12. There is reason to believe that, later on, such liberal injunctions were repealed. In any case, "in Latvia, the attempts of the priests to obtain land have been defeated" (A. 1940, No. 12).

(43) New York Times, June 30, 1941.

(44) Quoted from an article by Rev. H. S. Leiper in Living Church, October 15, 1941.

(45) New York Times, June 30, 1941.

(46) Wire from Kuibysheff to the Associated Press, December 28, 1941.

(47) New York Times, August 22, 1941.

(48) Ibid., October 1 and 7, 1941.

(49) Ibid., April 25, 1942.

(50) Ibid., October 7, 1941.

(51) Ibid., November 19, 1941

(52) Ibid., January 5, 1942.

(53)  *Ibid.*, April 6, 1942.

(54)  Quoted from the article mentioned *supra*, note 44.

(55)  *New York Times*, April 25, 1942.

(56)  I am indebted for this information to Rev. H. S. Leiper.

(57)  *New York Times*, April 25, 1942. See, however, in *New York Times*, May 4, 1942, a note on the activity of Bishop Polycarp of Luck, the head of an "autonomous council of Ukrainian bishops."

# CHAPTER SIX

# The Causes of the Change. The Outlook

THE EVENTS OF THE TWENTY-FOUR YEARS which have elapsed since the catastrophe of November 7, 1917, have not settled the controversy between Christian and Communist. Religion still lives in the hearts of millions of Russian people, old and young, illiterate and educated. Atheism, to be sure, has taken away other millions. A state of equilibrium has been reached, and the momentum of the anti-religious offensive has been exhausted. It has been broken by the adamant resistance of the believers. That *this* resistance could break *this* offensive is miraculous; for the offensive was maneuvered with determination, in consecutive waves, using new devices gradually invented and perfected by trial-and-error, by a dictatorial government which usually got what it wanted.

The devices for religious persecution have been (1) *direct violence:* (a) imprisonment or execution of clergymen and active laymen; (b) closure of churches by force, sometimes with the subsequent commandeering of the buildings for non-religious or even anti-religious assemblies; (c) destruction and desecration of icons and vessels; (2) *interference in Church life:* (a) depriving the churches of legal and economic means; (b) inhibiting normal relations between higher and lower levels of the hierarchy;

(c) helping to launch a schism, and (d) the prohibiting of the churches' charitable, cultural, and social activity; (3) *discrimination:* (a) against the clergy, official, and far-reaching, and (b) against active laymen, unofficial, but also very telling; (4) *eradication of religious education,* not only from schools, but everywhere else (even from churches), except for education within the family; (5) *organization of anti-religious propaganda:* (a) in schools and (b) throughout the country; and finally (6) *obstructing of pious customs* proper to the "Orthodox way of life."

Never were all these measures used simultaneously. Violence has been systematically used only during the three periods of outright attack (1922–23, 1929–30, and 1937–38). Of the other methods, that of fostering a schism was given up in the later twenties; legal discrimination against priests was dropped with the enactment of the Stalin Constitution in 1936. The restraints upon the Orthodox way of life were alleviated in 1934–35 and still more since 1939. The intensity of other methods has varied widely: anti-religious education is not as comprehensive as it was in 1930–34; anti-religious propaganda is not as barbarous as it was in the early thirties, and this is perhaps the most essential change instituted by the New Religious Policy. Cultural strangulation, which proved to be the most effective method invented by the Communists, no longer operates extensively. But the deprivation of religious associations of the right to own property, the trammeling of ecclesiastical administration, and at least partial discrimination against the believers have been kept up, despite all readjustments. And, as has been explained in Chapter Five, by abandoning certain devices, the government has not made up for past injuries; exiles or prisoners have not been released, closed churches have not been reopened, privileges to the Living Church have not been altogether curtailed.[1]

Once more, as in the early centuries of Christianity, faith has proved to be stronger than oppression. But it cannot be denied that organized religion has suffered more than religion as such: many people continue to believe, but do not dare show their beliefs by regular church attendance; many members of the Greek Orthodox Church have forsaken it and joined or organized sects; many, especially among the younger generation, desperately look for something better than the official Marxist line, but do not yet know the way to Christ. The religious dilemma is both discouraging and hopeful: discouraging because it is chaotic, hopeful because there is burning faith in some and a pathetic longing for faith in others.

By contrast, the position of anti-religion is altogether precarious. Twenty-four years of experimental atheism have shown to its proselytes that religion is not what it must be according to the erudite hypotheses of Marx, or their popularizations from which the majority of the anti-religious professors derive their wisdom. In religion they have met a strong and indomitable force, so strong that many Communists have begun to think it innate.

Moreover, the anti-Church or the Militant Atheists League has proved a wretched disappointment. By subsidies and privileges, its membership can be increased; but it is a dead body; no one any longer respects it. Belief has been destroyed in many, and many of the young people have been kept from God's word and God's servants. But "free of religious prejudice" has not materialized. Deprived of

God, they have taken up primitive magic which is ubiquitous and will appear wherever it is not dispelled by religion. No iron and enlightened "positivists," accepting nothing but quantitative science; rather, poor, primitive, superstitious men are marshalled against the followers of Christ.

**2**

An unfavorable balance, after twenty-four years of experimentation! This is well known to the Communist leaders and has played its part in their decision to launch the New Religious Policy. But the realization of the adverse balance has, obviously, only played *a* part in this decision, and there must be additional factors. We can see this is true because the failure has often been admitted by the Soviet leaders, in 1921, in 1923 (after the first attack), in 1928 (after the few years of relative let-up), in 1930 (immediately after the second attack), and so forth. Since set-backs were never attributed to the internal strength of religion, but always to unsatisfactory combative techniques, more or less substantial changes have followed each recognition, but never on such a scale as in 1939. Moreover, their force has varied: the Communists sometimes curbed the attack, but sometimes intensified it. Hence it may reasonably be assumed that in 1939, some strong additional factor urged the government to admit the necessity of a compromise.

This additional factor which was present in 1939, but not earlier, was the social and cultural revival which first showed its head in 1934 and, since, has acquired more and more momentum despite temporary interruptions which, once overcome, only make the wheel spin faster. In other words, the New Religious Policy cannot be understood as an isolated phenomenon, but only if it is viewed as part of a significant whole.

Sweeping alterations, almost incredible in a society which still calls itself Communist, have taken place in Russia since 1934.[2] First, Communist economics have been substantially qualified. The State is still almost the only business man of the country, producing and selling all industrial commodities and controlling agriculture. But the natural urge of men to improve their personal and domestic conditions by better work is no longer repressed as it was during the years of integral Communism (1929–1934). There is a great difference in the wages of skilled and unskilled labor, in the remuneration of good and poor work.[3] Creative work, both technical and artistic, entitles the producers to high honorary and cash awards.[4] There are no longer any ration cards to standardize consumption. Everyone is allowed to buy anything sold at the market; price discriminations have been abolished. Collective farms still exist but members are now allowed individually to cultivate allotments within the common lands and to possess cattle.[5] Stalin himself has voiced the necessity of furthering private interests together with the collective on the farm.[6]

Second, there is a movement towards making "national" the international Communist revolution, towards reconciling Communism and tradition. The development started with the abolition of "sociology," *i.e.,* of Marxist doctrine, in high schools (April 22 and 24, 1934). This step was immediately followed by an order to reintroduce courses in Russian History which had been altogether neglected for fifteen years, and to supplement relevant textbooks (May 16, 1934). In June, 1934, the readers of Soviet newspapers were astonished to find there words which seemed to have been forgotten, such as "fatherland," "patriotism," and "Russia." Russia was still proclaimed to be the fatherland of all workers of the world, but above all of the Russian people. The grandeur of this people and its history, its arts and literature were stressed wherever possible. Folk arts which had been officially described as a barbaric survival were lauded to the skies after the spectacular appearance of Stalin at a performance of peasant songs and dances on November 7, 1935. When the textbooks ordered in 1934 were finished, they were rejected by the government (January 27, 1936), for they were found to be unjust to Russian history; the glorious deeds of Muscovite princes who created the National State, the reforms of Peter the Great, the resistance of the people against Napoleon, the liberation of serfs by Emperor Alexander II, even the talents of generals who commanded Russian armies in 1914–17 merited praise. When, in 1937, the Pushkin centennial was celebrated, a slogan was circulated which well summarized the new feeling: Russia is a great nation because it gave the world Pushkin and Lenin. The symbol of Russian culture and the symbol of Communism, united in one formula: this is significant.

The movement spread to all fields of social and cultural life. The Communists rediscovered the family. Divorce is still easy, but frequent remarriage is officially frowned on and sometimes even indicted as rape. Abortion is no longer free. Desertion of wife and children and the neglect of invalid parents are considered intolerably petty bourgeois. Schools which for years had been "revolutionary youth clubs" where nothing was taught, have been given a conservative, even reactionary air: uniforms for pupils, yearly examinations, certificates and strict discipline, enforced by the headmaster, if necessary, with the help of police. The pre-revolutionary curriculum has been restored in its essentials, except for religion and classical languages.

People are no longer persuaded to wear rags; they are rather cautioned to be well dressed. Women copy "bourgeois" fashions, men wear starched collars, and the gorgeous uniforms of officers and soldiers suggest a resurrection of the Czars. And this impression is strengthened when one hears that these officers are addressed as lieutenants, colonels, even generals; both military men and civilians wear insignia of orders which, together with rank and title, had been abolished by the government as purely bourgeois.

Men and women are invited to enjoy life and not to sacrifice everything to social construction. And they are given means: the stage offers more classics than propaganda plays; at the movies, in addition to the usual foolishness, one may see entertaining Russian and foreign films. In addition to novels and short stories of *social realism* (eternal variations on "constructing socialism"), people may read European masterpieces, and modern historical novels, which are often well written and tend to glorify Russia's past. Historical plays and movies are common and popular.[7]

Third, there has been a Constitutional reform, the famous reform of 1936 which gave Russia "the most democratic constitution in the world." Truly, the reform has been a great disappointment for those who thought that the Russian dictatorship had abdicated in favor of democracy; for the dictatorship has not abdicated even a particle of its omnipotence.[8] However, it is plastered with democratic

slogans, and vigorous efforts have been made to persuade
the people that now they are free and rule themselves. The
reform was bogus; but even bogus reforms are significant:
they pose the question, why has the government acted
as though it intended to grant liberty?

In the great stream of events, religion was an obvious
snag. It is true that already in 1934–36, persecution was
somewhat lightened (Chapter II, section 6). But almost
without exception, the small concessions were merely reflec-
tions of those made in other fields, and the general attitude
of the government towards religion remained unchanged.
It may be assumed that in 1934–36, the government hoped
to achieve a compromise between the old and the new
culture in which the Communist doctrine would play the
role which under the Czars had belonged to religion. It
would be the cornerstone of culture.

This plan was doomed, *ab ovo*: culture is not a random
aggregate of elements, but a system in which all factors are
interdependent; [9] primary parts of a culture cannot be ar-
tificially switched. Since Russian culture is rooted in religion, to restore all its habiliments without religion was
absurd. What *was* possible was a crash of the restoration
or an inclusion of religion. Events of the last few years have
shown that the latter has been chosen for the time being.
Why did the Communist rulers bow to so embarrassing and
bitter an alternative? This question can only be answered if
we probe a little deeper and analyze the underlying causes
of the reaction.

A discussion of these causes may be conducted on two
levels, the abstract and the concrete. Abstractly, we may
say that all revolutions must in par. undo what they have

done if the society in which the revolution has taken place is to survive. This is the golden rule drawn by historians from the French revolutionary and of the post-revolutionary epochs: post-revolutionary France is a child both of the Revolution and of the *ancien régime*.

The outcome of the Russian revolution must be the same. Any vital society, after suffering an eruption, returns to the climate best suited to its nature and to its historical evolution. The Russian revolution succeeds wherever it continues historical tasks interrupted by war, civil war and their concomitant devastation. The industrialization cannot be gainsaid, but Russia had tended towards this since the 1890's. She is no longer illiterate, but a well-thought out program for mass education was in force as early as 1908, itself a crystallization of the previous efforts of the *Zemstvos*.[10]

On the contrary, all efforts to uproot Russia's historical culture and to plant a new, proletarian and international one have been blighted. Millions of neglected and delinquent children were the product of the destruction of the family and ancient morality. A fearful lowering of the cultural level, shown in what is called in contemporary Russia "technical illiteracy," has been the reward of the new school system, expected to alter the very nature of man. Defeatism has been the response to fifteen years of vilification of the fatherland. And the calamitous famines of 1922–23 and 1932–33 which have cost the country millions of human lives have been the result of unrestricted Communism in economics.[11]

The very logic of history forced the Communists either to retreat or to cede leadership to another group, after another revolution. Communists have always been able opportunists: in 1921, under similar circumstances, they preferred "a serious retreat for a long time ahead" to the distant threat of political breakdown. In the thirties, they once more preferred retreat to loss of power.

This is an abstract explanation which does not help us to understand why the retreat took place in 1934 and not earlier or later. A consideration of concrete events elucidates this timing.

The period of the great retrenchment (1934–41) coincided with a gradual bogging down in the Soviet's international relations. In 1931, Japan invaded Southern Manchuria, and, the next year, Northern Manchuria, close to the Soviet border. For the first time since 1920, a real threat of war appeared on the political horizon. However, this virtual war was merely colonial and did not menace the regime. In 1933, Hitler came into power in Germany and began his vociferous attack on Communism which, however, did not prevent him later from making his peace with the Soviet. At first, the permanence of Hitler's government was questioned; between Russia and Germany, there was Poland whose army, in 1933, was obviously stronger than the German. But in January, 1934, the German-Polish pact was signed. Then, the imminence of war was appreciated in Moscow, and the pact was understood as an alliance hostile to the Soviet State.

Marxist prophecies for once have been correct: in the long run, war between Communism and Fascism was inevitable. What was not and could not be conceded was that the very existence of Fascism was largely due to the foolish international policy of the Soviet in its first fifteen years. The threat of war, in the East and in the West, was a retaliation for the threat of revolution, in the East and in the West.

Never, since 1934, has the Communist government forgotten that war was ahead. Large scale military preparations were carried out which, in 1941, have made possible the almost unbelievable resistance of the Red Army. But another, equally important precaution was taken. The Communist government always knew that its policy was unpopular. Early in the thirties, the hope of a paradise on earth to be brought about by the First Five Year Plan appeared to be a grotesque delusion. Despair and defeatism were rampant [12] and this was natural among people deprived of any joy, any hope, any values. That did not matter in the eyes of the Communists, so long as no one could attack them. However, it began to matter very much when attack became possible, even probable. The most important step in a total preparation for war, consequently, was to solidify the nation with a new spirit.

This meant withdrawals—many, many withdrawals—beginning with cultural concessions which would restore national consciousness to a nation which its rulers had tried to denationalize. Through a fatal irony, excesses of internationalism outside had resulted in a recrudescence of nationalism within Communist Russia!

Concessions have been many, and we have already made a rapid survey of them. But how do we know that they were concessions and not steps in the government's gradual but basic acceptance of human values? We know it because all reforms have been half-reforms, repealing only so many of the revolutionary measures as seemed unavoidable. Thus, for instance, the abominable family laws of 1917–18 (with later amendments) have not been repealed, but have only been made slightly less stringent. Typical is the so-called Constitutional reform. Through it, Russia has not become a democracy; it bears witness, none the less, to the eagerness of the people to regain all that generations of Russians fought for before the catastrophe of November 7, 1917, and at the same time to the government's unwillingness to grant real freedom.

The concessions have produced the expected fruits: the Russians fight not only because they have arms, but also because once more they have something to fight for. It is uncanny what skillful propaganda can do, if it does not oppose but reenforces the natural aspirations of human beings. Russia has quickly found herself. Her traditions came to life and the Russians of 1941 have fought as their ancestors before them. It may be asserted that in 1941 they fight better than they would have fought in 1933 or even in 1939: time and compromise have worked for the new order.

The anticipations of the Communists were well founded and the events of 1941 may be used to explain much earlier decisions. But let us return to the time when compromises were new, to the time of the inauguration of the New Religious Policy.

At length Russia had, at least in many respects, to return to her customary ways. The structure of traditional culture made any restoration impossible that altogether left out religion. Developments outside, partly provoked by Communist policy, determined that the great retreat must take place in the later thirties of the twentieth century.

Now it must be explained why definite concessions to religion were made so late, and why they were interrupted by the atrocious attack of 1937–38. In the light of previous explanations, neither question is difficult. The series of concessions made by a reluctant government to a people with whom it had to come to terms must naturally be weighed in the governmental scale of values. As atheism is at the heart of Marxism, any concession to religion was much more difficult than concessions to art or to the popular desire for more abundant and varied economic goods. The very structure of Russian culture made a compromise with religion unavoidable: you cannot exalt the *gesta* of Russian rulers and omit the historical role of the Church; you cannot read Russian classics—and this reading is now imposed on the youth—and ignore theological and philosophical problems with which these works are loaded. But time was needed to see this; therefore, the arrival of the New Religious Policy was tardy.

The reluctance of the government to yield to religion explains the last persecution. Was it not possible, thought the Communists, to avoid the concessions by exterminating the enemy to whom concessions were to be made? Experience should have warned them that it was impossible. But it is a truism that historical lessons are rarely understood by those who receive them. From 1936 to 1938, a temptation to try once more the tactics of extermination was combined with the policy of concessions. It was the time of the great purge, of the famous Moscow trials which resulted in the execution of all that remained of the Old Guard of Communism, and the liquidation of the leaders of the Red Army. The thesis was obviously this: concessions are necessary, but concessions are always dangerous, because they provoke new demands and provide an excellent opportunity for the rise of new leadership; therefore, concessions must be offset by the wiping out of potential leaders. Where could they be found? Theoretically, within the highest ranks of the Communist Party; among the Red generals, and among the leaders of the Church. Such suppositions are born out by the fact that in 1937–38, the attack on religion was especially directed against the clergy, while the rank and file was unmolested.

The liquidation of the Old Guard did not make much noise in Russia: in their hearts, people did not distinguish between the men murdered by Stalin and Stalin himself. The execution of Red generals was probably resented in the army, and therefore had to be followed up by the dismissal of tens of thousands of officers. But the attack on the clergy once more inflamed religious resentment. The government did not have to make concessions to atone for the great purge. But the attack on religion cried for expiation—the government wanted popular support and the people rebelled against anti-clericalism.


### 3

Cannot the New Religious Policy be looked on as the precursor of further concessions, leading to the restoration of religious freedom? The statement of the question brings to light enormous difficulties. As a well-informed Russian writer has recently written: "To begin with, the Soviet government, without losing its prestige, cannot grant religious freedom to the people of the Union simply because such freedom officially exists. Moreover, the process of granting religious freedom to Soviet citizens is more than complicated. If the Soviet government were to yield . . . it would have to disband the Atheists League . . . It would have to allow the Russian Church to call a Council for the election of a Patriarch. It would have to give permission to reopen religious academies, seminaries, and schools. It would have to return to worshippers at least some of the churches, long ago converted into dance halls and museums. It must give assurance to the population that their church attendance will not handicap their state jobs . . . To grant all these reforms, the very idea of Communism will be defeated." [13]

For, as the Orthodox bishops, exiled to the concentration camp on the Solovetski islands, declared (see Chapter II, section 5) as early as the summer of 1926, "The Church wants religion to flourish, Communism wants it to perish. With such a deep chasm in fundamental principles separating the Church and the State, it becomes impossible that the inner harmonies of reconciliation should obtain. There can be no reconciliation between assertion and negation, between Yes and No. For the very soul of the Church, the reason of its being, is just what is categorically denied by Communism." [14]

Religious freedom in Russia, so long as Communists continue to rule, is impossible. This is a fact which has brought and continues to bring on crises in the relations of the Soviet Union with other countries. The oppression of religion was one of the stumbling blocks to a formal American recognition of the USSR. When, in 1933, negotiations were opened in Washington, the President received hundreds of letters and telegrams reminding him of this fact. This became a matter of concern in Russia, and even the Soviet press was obliged to notice the American protests.[15] The question came up in connection with a stipulation that citizens of the United States enjoy the same freedom of conscience and religion in Russia as at home. No special liberty was promised to Americans, since it was asserted that the existing Soviet legislation guaranteed it. Nevertheless, the Administration expected its friendly admonitions to bear fruit. A minister was sent to Moscow along with officials and business men. They did not stay long: the hopes of both missions were disappointed.

The difficulty came up again soon after the outbreak of the Russo-German war with the decision of the Administration of the United States to help the USSR. This time, the problem involved the moral consequences of relieving, in the advance of a common enemy, a State whose fundamental principles are the antithesis of the American way of life. The outcome was that President Roosevelt was urged to take advantage of the unique opportunity and obtain for the Russian people at least one of the four freedoms.

It is apparent that American diplomacy has exhorted the Soviet Government to grant religious freedom as a means of tempting the American public to give its all-out support.[16] A vivid discussion of the question arose when Mr. Hull made public a letter from the Polish ambassador. According to this, complete freedom of worship is permitted to Polish soldiers who enlist in Russia for service against Hitler; Catholic chaplains accompany the regiments; a Polish Catholic Church and a synagogue have been reopened in Moscow.[17]

The upshot proved as anti-climactic as it had been in

1933. On October 5, 1941, a Soviet spokesman commented on the American proposals:

"In the Soviet Union, the Church is separated from the State. This means that the State gives no advantages to this or that religion and does not support mosques, churches, or synagogues. Citizens adhering to a certain religion maintain their religious institutions at their own expense. There is freedom of worship in the USSR. This means that any Soviet citizen may adhere to any religion; this is a matter for the conscience of each citizen. There is the Old Greek Orthodox Church in the USSR, and also the New Greek Orthodox Church, the Old Believers, the Armenian Church, the Molokan Church, the Dukhobors, Moslems, Evangelists, Baptists, Seventh Day Adventists, Jews, Roman Catholics, Lutherans, Buddhists, and others. Religion is a private affair for the Soviet citizen in which the State does not interfere and considers it unnecessary to interfere. The Soviet Constitution provides not only the right to adhere to this or that religion, but also the right of Soviet citizens not to belong to any church and to conduct anti-religious propaganda. Soviet law does not consider it possible to force citizens to worship according to either this or that religion. This is a matter for the conscience of each Soviet citizen. The Constitution of the USSR is based on the following: Freedom to worship according to any religion assumes that religion, church, or congregation will not be utilized for overthrow of the existing regime recognized in the country." The declaration was closed by reading the text of the famous Article 124.[18]

Then Mr. Lozovsky answered correspondents' questions, declaring that to raise the issue of religious liberty in the

USSR was much ado about nothing, and that many of those who raised it refused to understand the Soviet's attitude. He said that the anti-religious museums would continue to function as a part of man's cultural history and that they belonged in the same category as an astronomical planetarium.[19]

The reaffirmation of Russia's "Constitutional" stand on religion was declared by the Very Reverend Edmund Walsh, S.J., to be tantamount to scotching President Roosevelt's hopes that true freedom of religion might be tolerated.[20]

### 4

After a few days of excitement, the issue of religious freedom in Russia was forgotten as issues are which appear to be not too vital, and for which no immediate solution seems likely. But the episode remains highly illuminating. Even in the course of a supreme ordeal, and under the friendly pressure of a mighty ally, the Communist government has not granted religious freedom but has been satisfied with a few minor concessions (Chapter V, section 3). It is more and more apparent that "Stalin cannot reverse the fixed policy of more than twenty years and allow not merely freedom of worship which exists in Russia in the sense that churches are still open, but freedom to teach religion, without opening the way to other revolutionary changes. For liberty, like peace and war, is indivisible. It is impossible to grant freedom of worship without granting freedom of speech, freedom of the press, freedom of assembly. Religious liberty cannot exist without civil liberty, and vice versa." [21]

What, then, is the outlook for religion in Russia? It depends largely on the outcome of the war. If the Soviet government is crushed by Germany or, if in the course of the war, it is replaced by a democratic government, the religious problem will be altogether different from the one studied in this work.[22] However, two decisive factors will determine the situation even in these contingencies: (1) religion is still there; and (2) the ancient organization of religion has been substantially shaken.

If the Soviet government survives the war and remains free to act according to its own inclinations, the same factors will be present. It is impossible to guess what its attitude towards religion will be. Never forget that the New Religious Policy is merely a compromise, reluctantly accepted for compelling reasons, and contrary to the convictions of the government. Hence, the concessions are precarious. If conditions alter to the advantage of the Communist government, a return to the policy of direct attack is possible with perhaps a general imposition of pressure along the whole "ideological front." But such relapses will not necessarily take place. The new cultural regime is pleasanter for the Communists themselves than the puritanical austerities of the thirties. Perhaps they will want to maintain it, and if they choose, perhaps religion will continue to enjoy not liberty, not even tolerance, but an easing off along the lines of 1939–41. Late in December, 1941, the Archbishop of Samara told a representative of the Associated Press that the members of the Greek Orthodox Church were no longer hostile to the Soviet government and that, in his opinion, no change in the State-Church relationship would take place after the war.[23]

This shows the rashness of an *ex cathedra* forecast of

future developments. Conflicting forces are at issue and can give impetus to one or the other of opposed tendencies, either renewed persecution or continued leniency and compromise. Let us, therefore, wind up on an intentionally unscientific note and recall an allegory of the later Middle Ages, the legend of a mythical town called *Grad Kitezh*. It was a godly town and when the Tartars, barbaric pagans, overran Russia, the town was allowed to sink into a lake, and all its church bells rang. It was to reappear when the Holy Faith was again free. And it did reappear: Russia herself became the *Grad Kitezh* and came to be known as "Holy Russia," through her faith in Christ. Now Russia is once more the invisible *Grad Kitezh*: church bells ring out only to the spiritual ears of believers, and church songs are now but a whisper. But why should it not be possible for history to repeat itself and for Holy Russia to rise once more from her baptism of blood?

### FOOTNOTES TO CHAPTER SIX

(1) One of the reasons for supporting the Living Church despite its complete failure within Russia is perhaps its usefulness outside Russia as an instrument for taking over the property of the Russian Orthodox Church in foreign countries. The most famous case is that of the transfer to the Living Church of the St. Nicholas Cathedral in New York.

(2) On the policy of concessions see A. Gide, *Retour de l'URSS*, Paris, 1936; Sir Walter Citrine, *I Search for Truth in Russia*, London, 1936; L. Trotsky, *Revolution Betrayed*, New York, 1937; and Sir Bernard Pares, *Russia*, Penguin Books, 1940.

(3) The differential has been introduced by means of the Stakhanoff movement (see above, Chapter II, note 74). About the curious procedure used by the Soviet government cf. my article "Le Stakhanovisme," *Russie et Chrétienté* (published by the "Centre Dominicain d'études russes"), 1936, No. 4.

(4) Mr. Dounayevsky, a composer of popular songs, is said to re-

ceive rubles 1,500 ($300) a day. *Cf.* K. London, *The Seven Soviet Arts,* New Haven, 1938, p. 37.

(5) *Cf.* my article "Structural Changes in Rural Russia," *Rural Sociology,* 2 (1937), pp. 24–27.

(6) P., March 12, 1935.

(7) *Cf.* H. W. Dana, "Patriotic Plays in Soviet Russia," *Russian Review,* 1 (1941), pp. 65–73, and H. Isvolsky, "Latest Trends in Soviet Literature," *ibid.,* pp. 74–80.

(8) *Cf.* my paper, "The Soviet Constitution," *Thought,* 16 (1941), pp. 627–44.

(9) P. Sorokin, *Social and Cultural Dynamics,* Vol. 4, N. Y., 1941, pp. 97 ff.

(10) In Imperial Russia, the Zemstvos were local self-governmental bodies which took care of public education, public health, highways, etc.

(11) *Cf.* my paper, "The Population of Soviet Russia," *Rural Sociology,* 5 (1940), pp. 308–9.

(12) About that time, the present writer had the opportunity to read hundreds of letters mailed from Russia in which these attitudes were well expressed.

(13) From a letter to the Editor of *New York Herald Tribune,* by Mr. A. Tarsaidze (*New York Herald Tribune,* October 10, 1941).

(14) However, the same bishops insisted on the necessity of a loyal application of the principle of the separation of State and Church; their message was directed against Acting Patriarch Sergius who looked for a compromise with the Communist government. *Cf.* Miliukoff (see Selected Bibliography), pp. 192–5.

(15) P., November 14, 1933.

(16) *New York Times,* September 16, 1941.

(17) *Ibid.,* October 1, 1941.

(18) This article has been commented on by Yaroslavsky as follows: "The Constitution (article 124) underlines the necessity of anti-religious propaganda." (*On anti-religious propaganda,* in Russian, Moscow, 1937.)

(19) *New York Times,* October 6, 1941.

(20) *Ibid.,* October 6, 1941.

(21) Ann O'Hare McCormick, in *New York Times,* October 6, 1941.

(22) From an appeal of Acting Patriarch Sergius (*New York Times,* February 22, 1942) it appears that, in the occupied part of Russia, German authorities tried to establish an "autonomous" Greek Orthodox Church which would be entirely subservient to the Nazis; such attempts are severely condemned by Sergius.

(23) Wire from Kuibysheff (Samara) to the Associated Press, December 28, 1941.

# Index

## I. GEOGRAPHICAL NAMES

## II. PERSONS

## III. SUBJECT MATTERS